CONTEMPORARY CRITICS

OF

EDUCATION

79-93

CONTEMPORARY CRITICS

OF

EDUCATION

Howard Ozmon

Chairman
Department of Education
Chicago State College

The Interstate
Printers & Publishers, Inc.

Danville, Illinois

Criticism carried to the height worthy of it, is a majestic office, perhaps an art, perhaps even a church.

—Walt Whitman

A critic is a man whose watch is five minutes ahead of other people's watches.

—Sainte-Beuve

CONTENTS

INTRODUCTION

The purpose of this book is to present some of the major criticisms being leveled at contemporary education at the preschool level through graduate school. All but five of the critics presented in this book are living writers who are very much concerned with the aims and methods of contemporary American education, and what they have to say needs to be seriously pondered by all of those concerned with the future of both public and private education in this country.

It is often true that the critic, particularly if he is considered "outside" of the profession he is criticizing, as some in this book are, is all too often looked upon as an interloper or as a negative person whose only claim to fame is that he attacks established aims and methods. It needs to be pointed out, however, that this is both a narrow and erroneous view of what the critic's role really is. It is true that one of the functions of the critic is to point out what he or she feels are educational shortcomings in our society, but the critic is also one who delivers praise where praise is due, and there are critics in this book who find much to praise as well as condemn in contemporary education. There is also much to obtain, I think, from an appraisal of education by those who are not necessarily a part of the educational establishment, and so necessary is the work they do that if they did not exist we should probably have to invent them. The function of the critic is primarily to analyze, and such an analysis may be done by admirals, businessmen, and scholars in diverse fields, as well as by professional educators. As many of these writers have achieved a wide and popular following, it makes it more imperative that we know something of their views, and this book was written to present the reader with a synthesis of some of the major criticisms currently being directed toward the schools.

This book has been arranged in a manner that presents each critic in a separate section. There is in each section a brief statement about the author's life, writings, and major educational criticisms, followed by a selection from one of his works highlighting in his own words what he feels to be right and wrong with contemporary education.

Someone once remarked that education is too serious a field to be left only to professional educators, and the critics in this book perform a much needed task in looking at education by-and-large without encumbrances or vested interests. Hopefully this book will serve to make all of those concerned with contemporary education more aware of the need for a constant on-going analysis of educational aims and methods, and hopefully also, to become critics themselves.

H. O.

MORTIMER J. ADLER

Mortimer J. Adler was born on December 28, 1902, in New York City. He attended DeWitt Clinton High School but dropped out at 15 after a difference with the principal. He went to work for the New York *Sun*, and in 1920 obtained a scholarship to Columbia University. Although Adler finished the four year course in three years and received a Phi Beta Kappa key, he refused to take the required swimming test and was not awarded a B.A.

Adler continued his course work at Columbia. As a graduate student he taught philosophy, as well as the famous General Honors Course. He received his Ph.D. in psychology from Columbia in 1928.

Adler taught at the University of Chicago under Robert Hutchins, as well as at St. John's College in Annapolis, Maryland. He collaborated with Hutchins in reprinting the Great Books in a complete set, and was instrumental in developing the Syntopicon as an index to the main ideas of the Great Books. In 1952 Adler became the founder of the Institute for Philosophical Research in Chicago, Illinois, of which he is now president.

Adler has written a number of books about education, including *How to Read a Book: The Art of Getting a Liberal Education* and, with Peter Wolff, *A General Introduction to the Great Books and to a Liberal Education.*

Although he studied under John Dewey as an undergraduate, Adler has been a fierce opponent of pragmatic philosophy. His philosophical views are more in the neo-Platonic and Thomistic tradition, and he strongly supports the moral and intellectual system of St. Thomas as an antidote to what he feels is a chaotic twentieth-century culture.

Adler, like Robert M. Hutchins, has championed a "Great Books" approach in American education as a way of cultivating and disciplining the mind. Most of our problems, he feels, are old ones in new forms, and unless we understand the great ideas of the past we will only wallow in a sea of confusion. Adler believes that only a liberal education such as the classics provide can really enrich our lives and make us rational and free.

HOW TO READ A BOOK

Mortimer J. Adler

As far back as I can remember, there have been complaints about the schools for not teaching the young to write and speak well. The complaints have focused mainly on the products of high school and college. An elementary school diploma never was expected to certify great competence in these matters. But after four or eight more years in school, it seemed reasonable to hope for a disciplined ability to perform these basic acts. English courses were, and for the most part still are, a staple ingredient in the high school curriculum. Until recently, freshman English was a required course in every college. These courses were supposed to develop skill in writing the mother tongue. Though less emphasized than writing, the ability to speak clearly, if not with eloquence, was also supposed to be one of the ends in view.

The complaints came from all sources. Businessmen, who certainly did not expect too much, protested the incompetence of the youngsters who came their way after school. Newspaper editorials by the score echoed their protests and added a voice of their own, expressing the misery of the educator who had to blue-pencil the stuff college graduates passed across his desk.

Teachers of freshman English in college have had to do over again what should have been completed in high school. Teachers of other college courses have complained about the impossibly sloppy and incoherent English which students hand in on term papers or examinations.

And anyone who has taught in the graduate school or in a law school knows that a B.A. from our best colleges means very little with ref-

Mortimer J. Adler. *How to Read a Book*, Simon & Schuster, Inc., New York, 1940, pp. 65-100. Copyright, © 1940, 1966, by Mortimer J. Adler. Reprinted by permission of Simon & Schuster, Inc.

erence to a student's skill in writing or speaking. Many a candidate for the Ph.D. has to be coached in the writing of his dissertation, not from the point of view of scholarship or scientific merit but with respect to the minimum requirements of simple, clear, straightforward English. My colleagues in the law school frequently cannot tell whether a student does or does not know the law because of his inability to express himself coherently on a point of issue.

I have mentioned only writing and speaking, not reading. Until very recently, no one paid much attention to the even greater and more prevalent incompetence in reading, except, perhaps, the law professors who, ever since the introduction of the case method of studying law, have realized that half the time in a law school must be spent in teaching the student how to read cases. They thought, however, that this burden rested peculiarly on them, that there was something very special about reading cases. They did not realize that if college graduates had a decent skill in reading, the more specialized technique of reading cases could be acquired in much less than half the time now spent.

One reason for the comparative neglect of reading and the stress on writing and speaking is a point I have already mentioned. Writing and speaking are, for most people, so much more clearly *activities* than reading is. Since we associate skill with ability, it is a natural consequence of this error to attribute defects in writing and speaking to lack of technique, and to suppose that failure in reading must be due to moral defect—to lack of industry rather than of skill. The error is gradually being corrected. More and more attention is being paid to the problem of reading. I do not mean that the educators have yet discovered what to do about it, but they have finally realized that the schools are failing just as badly, if not worse, in the matter of reading, as in writing and speaking.

It should be obvious at once that these skills are related. They are all arts of using language in the process of communication, whether initiating it or receiving it. We should not be surprised, therefore, if we find a positive correlation among defects in these several skills. Without the benefit of scientific research by means of educational measurements, I would be willing to predict that someone who cannot write well cannot read well either. In fact, I would go further. I would wager that his inability to read is partly responsible for his defects in writing.

How difficult it may be to read, it is easier than writing and speaking well. To communicate well to others, one must know how communications are received, and be able, in addition, to master the medium to produce the desired effects. Though the arts of teaching and being taught are correlative, the teacher, either as writer or speaker, must pre-vision the process of being taught in order to direct it. He must, in short, be able to read what he writes, or listen to what he says, as if he were being taught by it. When teachers themselves do not possess the art of being taught, they cannot be very good teachers.

I do not have to ask you to accept my unsupported prediction or to meet my wager in the blind. The experts can be called to testify in the light of scientific evidence. The product of our schools has been mea-sured by the accredited apparatus of achievement tests. These tests touch all sorts of academic accomplishment—standard areas of infor-mation, as well as the basic skills, the three R's. They show not only that the high school graduate is unskilled but also that he is shockingly un-informed. We must confine our attention to defects of skill, especially to reading, although the findings on writing and speaking are supporting evidence that the high school graduate is generally at sea when it comes to any aspect of communication.

This is hardly a laughing matter. However deplorable it may be that those who have gone through twelve years of schooling should lack rudimentary information, how much more so is it that they should be disbarred from using the only means that can remedy the situation. If they could read—not to mention write and speak—they might be able to inform themselves throughout their adult life.

Notice that the defect which the tests discover is in the easier type of reading—reading for information. For the most part, the tests do not even measure ability to read for understanding. If they did, the results would cause a riot.

Last year Professor James Mursell, of Columbia's Teachers College, wrote an article in *The Atlantic Monthly*, entitled "The Defeat of the Schools." He based his allegation on "thousands of investigations" which comprise the "consistent testimony of thirty years of enormously varied research in education." A large mass of evidence comes from a recent survey of the schools of Pennsylvania carried on by the Carnegie Foun-dation. Let me quote his own words:

> What about English? Here, too, there is a record of failure and defeat. Do pupils in school learn to read their mother tongue effectively? Yes and no. Up to the fifth and sixth grade, reading, on the whole, is effectively taught and well learned. To that level

we find a steady and general improvement but beyond it the curves flatten out to a dead level. This is not because a person arrives at his natural limit of efficiency when he reaches the sixth grade, for it has been shown again and again that with special tuition much older children, and also adults, can make enormous improvement. Nor does it mean that most sixth-graders read well enough for all practical purposes. A great many pupils do poorly in high school because of sheer ineptitude in getting meaning from the printed page. They can improve; they need to improve; but they don't.

The average high school graduate has done a great deal of reading, and if he goes on to college he will do a great deal more; but he is likely to be a poor and incompetent reader. (Note that this holds true of the *average* student, not the person who is subject for special remedial treatment.) He can follow a simple piece of fiction and enjoy it. But put him up against a closely written exposition, a carefully and economically stated argument, or a passage requiring critical consideration, and he is at a loss. It has been shown, for instance, that the average high school student is amazingly inept at indicating the central thought of a passage, or the levels of emphasis and subordination in an argument or exposition. To all intents and purposes he remains a sixth grade reader till well along in college.

Even after he has finished college, I must add, he is not much better. I think it is true that no one can get through college who cannot read for information with reasonable efficiency. It may even be that he could not get into college were he thus deficient. But if we keep in mind the distinction between the types of reading, and remember that the tests measure primarily the ability to do the simpler sort, we cannot take much consolation from the fact that college students read better than sixth-graders. Evidence from the graduate and professional schools tends to show that, so far as reading for understanding is concerned, they are still sixth-graders.

Professor Mursell writes even more dismally of the range of reading in which the schools succeed in engaging the interest of students. It is somewhat sanguine to talk about students and graduates reading the great books, when it appears that they do not read even the good non-fiction books which come out every year.

I pass rapidly over Mursell's further report of the facts about writing: that the average student cannot express himself "clearly, exactly, and correctly in his native tongue"; that "a great many high school pupils are not able to discriminate between what is a sentence and what is not"; that the average student has an impoverished vocabulary. "As one goes from senior year in high school to senior year in college, the vocabulary content of written English hardly seems to increase at all. After twelve years in school a great many students still use English in many respects childish and undeveloped; and four years more bring slight improvement." These facts have a bearing on reading. The student who cannot "express fine and precise shades of meaning" certainly cannot detect them in the expression of anyone else who is trying to communicate above the level of subtlety which a sixth-grader can grasp.

There is more evidence to cite. Recently the Board of Regents of New York State solicited an inquiry into the achievement of its schools. This was carried out by a commission under the supervision of Professor Luther Bulick of Columbia. One of the volumes of the report treats of the high schools, and in this a section is devoted to the "command of the tools of learning." Let me quote again:

> Large numbers even of the high school graduates are serious-ly deficient in the basic tools of learning. The tests given to leaving pupils by the Inquiry included a test of ability to read and understand straightforward English... The passages presented to the pupils consisted of paragraphs taken from simple scientific articles, historical accounts, discussions of economic problems, and the like. The test was originally constructed for eighth grade pupils.

They discovered that the average high-school senior could pass a test designed to measure an achievement proper in the eighth grade. This is certainly not a remarkable victory for the high schools. But they also discovered that "a disturbingly large proportion of New York State boys and girls leave the secondary schools,—even go on to higher schools,—without having attained a desirable minimum." One must agree with their sentiment when they say that "in skills which everyone must use"—such as reading and writing—"everyone should have at least a minimum of competence." It is clear that Professor Mursell is not using language too strong when he speaks of "the defeat of the schools."

The Regents' Inquiry investigated the kind of learning which high-school students do by themselves, apart from school and courses. This, they rightly thought, could be determined by their out-of-school reading. And they tell us, from their results, "that once out of school, most boys and girls read solely for recreation, chiefly in magazines of mediocre or inferior fiction and in daily newspapers." The range of their reading, in school and out, is woefully slight and of the simplest and poorest sort. Nonfiction is out of the question. They are not even acquainted with the best novels published during their years in school. They know the names only of the most obvious best sellers. Worse than that, "once out of school, they tend to let books alone." Fewer than 40 per cent of the boys and girls interviewed had read any book or any part of a book in the two weeks preceding the interviews. Only one in ten had read non-fiction books. For the most part, they read magazines, if anything. And here the level of their reading is low: "fewer than two people in a hundred read magazines of the type of Harper's, Scribner's, or The Atlantic Monthly."

What is the cause of this shocking illiteracy? The Regents' Inquiry report points its finger at the heart of the trouble when it says that "the reading habits of these boys and girls are no doubt directly affected by the fact that many of them have never learned to read understandingly." Some of them "apparently felt that they were completely educated, and that reading was therefore unnecessary." But, for the most part, they do not know how to read, and therefore do not enjoy reading. The possession of skill is an indispensable condition of its use and of enjoyment in its exercise. In the light of what we know about their general inability to read—for understanding and even, in some cases, for information—it is not surprising to discover the limited range of reading among high-school graduates, and the poor quality of what they do read.

The serious consequences are obvious. "The inferior quality of reading done by large numbers of these boys and girls," this section of the Regents' report concludes, "offers no great hope that their independent reading will add very much to their educational stature." Nor, from what we know of the achievement in college, is the hope for the college graduate much greater. He is only a little more likely to do much serious reading after he graduates, because he is only a little more skilled in reading after four more years spent in educational institutions.

I want to repeat, because I want you to remember, that however distressing these findings may seem, they are not half as bad as they would be if the tests were themselves more severe. The tests measure a relatively simple grasp of relatively simple passages. The questions the students being measured must answer after they have read a short paragraph call for very little more than a precise knowledge of what the writer said. They do not demand much in the way of interpretation, and almost nothing of critical judgment.

I say that the tests are not severe enough, but the standard I would set is certainly not too stringent. Is it too much to ask that a student be able to read a whole book, not merely a paragraph, and report not only what was said therein but show an increased understanding of the subject matter being discussed? Is it too much to expect from the schools that they train their students not only to interpret but to criticize; that is, to discriminate what is sound from error and falsehood, to suspend judgment if they are not convinced, or to judge with reason if they agree or disagree? I hardly think that such demands would be exorbitant to make of high school or college, yet if such requirements were incorporated into tests, and a satisfactory performance were one of the conditions of graduation, not one in a hundred students now getting their diplomas each June would wear the cap and gown.

You may think that the evidence I have so far presented is local, being restricted to New York and Pennsylvania, or that it places too much weight on the average or poorer high school student. That is not the case. The evidence represents what is going on in the country generally. The schools of New York and Pennsylvania are better than average. And the evidence includes the best high school seniors, not merely the poorer ones.

Let me support this last statement by one other citation. In June, 1939, the University of Chicago held a four-day conference on reading for teachers attending the summer session. At one of the meetings, Professor Diederich, of the Department of Education, reported the results of a test given at Chicago to top-notch high school seniors who came there from all parts of the country to compete for scholarships. Among other things, these candidates were examined in reading. The results, Professor Diederich told the thousand teachers assembled, showed that most of these very "able" students simply could not understand what they read.

Moreover, he went on to say, "our pupils are not getting very much direct help in understanding what they read or hear, or in knowing what they mean by what they say or write." Nor is the situation limited to high schools. It applies equally to colleges in this country, and even in England, as indicated by the recent researches of Mr. I. A. Richards concerning the linguistic skill of undergraduates in Cambridge University.

Why are the students not getting any help? It cannot be because the professional educators are unaware of the situation. That conference at Chicago ran for four days—with many papers presented at morning, afternoon, and evening sessions—all on the problem of reading. It must be because the educators simply do not know what to do about it; in addition, perhaps, because they do not realize how much time and effort must be expended to teach students how to read, write, and speak well. Too many other things, of much less importance, have come to clutter up the curriculum.

Some years ago I had an experience which is illuminating in this connection. Mr. Hutchins and I had undertaken to read the great books with a group of high school juniors and seniors in the experimental school which the university runs. This was thought to be a novel "experiment" or worse, a wild idea. Many of these books were not being read by college juniors and seniors. They were reserved for the delectation of graduate students. And we were going to read them with high school boys and girls!

At the end of the first year, I went to the principal of the high school to report on our progress. I said that these youngsters were clearly interested in reading the books. The questions they asked showed that. The acuteness and vitality of their discussion of matters raised in class showed that they had enough intelligence to do the work. In many respects, they were better than older students who had been dulled by years of listening to lectures, taking notes, and passing examinations. They had much more edge than college seniors or graduate students. But, I said, it was perfectly obvious that they did not know how to read a book. Mr. Hutchins and I, in the few hours a week we had with them, could not discuss the books and also teach them how to read. It was a shame that their native talents were not being trained to perform a function that was plainly of the highest educational importance.

JACQUES BARZUN

Jacques Barzun was born on November 30, 1907, in Creteil, France. He was the son of a literary scholar, Henri Martin Barzun, and spent his boyhood among some of the foremost novelists and artists of Paris. He attended the French Lycée Janson de Sailly, and in 1917 came to America with his father who was sent here on a diplomatic mission.

Barzun entered Columbia University in 1923 and finished at the head of his class in 1927. During these years he wrote for various college publications, as well as for other magazines such as *Vanity Fair*. He received an M.A. degree from Columbia in 1928, and his Ph.D. in history in 1932. He began his teaching career at Columbia, and became a full professor of history in 1945. In 1955 he became Dean of the Graduate Faculties at Columbia, a position he held until 1967.

Barzun has written several books in the area of education and history, and some of his most notable writings on education are *The House of Intellect*, *Teacher in America*, and *The American University*.

Barzun feels that there is a lot that is wrong with our manners, as well as with our social and political life, and that much of it is due to our faulty educational system. He feels that if we really want to make education better we must forget the sloganeering of mass education, and remember that education is not schooling but a lifelong process encouraged by the desire to lead a good life.

Barzun feels that in trying to school everyone, we have tended to make allowances for poor work and low standards. He feels that we have degraded intellect to the point that one may even try to hide it, even though more people are being "educationed" than ever before. Barzun believes that an educated person is one who has learned how to use the language, and one who uses it in ways that improve both himself and those with whom he comes in contact.

THE HOUSE OF INTELLECT

Jacques Barzun

Clearly, the blame for much that is lacking or painful in our manners can be laid upon our education, individual and collective. The same cause will also explain what is wrong with our politics and ways of business, with our press and public opinion. Indeed, whatever is wrong is the fault of the schools, for is it not there that we learn to become what we are? This common indictment overlooks but one point, which is that the schools are run by adults—and run to suit other adults in political, intellectual, or business life. The schools are thus as fully the product of our politics, business, and public opinion as these are the products of our schools. It is because the link is so close that the schools are so hard to change.

They are, for the same reason, hard to describe, showing as they do the diversity and elusiveness of culture itself. Because it is thought of as a sheltered place invaded by worldlings, the school is often forgiven for resembling the world; it is always possible to say, "That is society's doing, not the school's." But this only proves that the best of schools can be no more than half-innocent. They work with spoiled materials: teachers marred by the ugly world and children already stamped with the defects that their parents condone by habit or foster on principle.

From these facts one great truth emerges: there is, there can be, no such thing as a good school.

The conclusion is repellent to our desire of perfection, but it is inescapable. It does not mean that all schools are bad: some are better than others; but none will do what in our naive fancy we liken to the work of an instrument of precision functioning independently of its makers. Any school has a system, and its action is therefore that of a cookie cutter carelessly handled. Schools that repudiate system as harsh and unjust turn out anarchical and more unjust. That is why the profoundest theorist of modern education, Rousseau, limited his scheme to one child and a tutor. Rousseau begins by pointing out that the story of Emile is not a model, but an ideal case that suggests new intentions rather than new practices. It is not imitable, if only because the tutor is a genius who devotes all his time and thought to a pupil who is unnaturally responsive.

Today, the Western world is at the other extreme from this situation. It is headed toward mass schooling, the European half of that world making the attempt some sixty years after the United States. Our current discussion of education in America is thus of peculiar interest, because we, dissatisfied with our handiwork, are seeking to change just at the time when England, France, and Germany are courageously starting to repeat our mistakes.[1] Our words and acts are doubly important because we are the pioneers others copy or listen to.

Ours is surely the most remarkable of educational systems in that it is the only one to deal with anything like the same numbers with so much liberality and persistence. We offer education from infancy to— I was about to say "the grave." Education in the United States is a passion and a paradox. Millions want it and commend it, and are busy about it, at the same time they are willing to degrade it by trying to get it free of charge and free of work. Education with us has managed to reconcile the contradictory extremes of being a duty and a diversion, and to elude intellectual control so completely that it can become an empty ritual without arousing protest.

Not that we have ever been satisfied with our schools. Long before the postwar self-searching, thousands of meetings and millions of words were being spent each year in debating improvements. But our characteristic softness then and now invests the whole attempt and reduces it for the most part to abstract worry and repetitious piety. The *doyen* of

---

[1] For a sample of foreign discussions, see in *The Listener* the protracted controversy on "The Child-Centered School" from April, 1957 to February, 1958; also in the Supplements to the German weekly *Das Parlament* for January 22 and 29, an essay of over fifty pages by Einrich Weinstock on the responsibility of the schools in an age of democracy and technology. Finally, see the three issues of *Education in France* published by the cultural services of the French Embassy, New York, 1957-58.

educational theorists in this country,[2] addressing in 1955 the Middle Atlantic States Philosophy of Education Association, opened his remarks with the words: "There is urgent need, current need for a broader and more effective education."[3] Last year, another critic, whose words make him representative of many others, expressed alarm at the insufficiency of present-day teaching in science. Did he suggest something to do, now as soon as possible? No. He asked for a "broad concept." A third lecturer, a well-known businessman, who knows the general resistance to intellectual subjects, wants to turn the present outcry to use by strengthening the universities' public position. Excellent. But what does he, an expert in "public relations," set forth as his main point? Defining goals: "The broad role of the institution must be defined." He does after a bit speak of curriculum, higher faculty salaries, and new buildings; but he soon relapses into "broad" ideas: "Creative thinking and creative teachers must, it seems to me, be given primary importance in defining the goals of any institution."[4] Read any segment of the press, lay or learned, and you will find that the angry protests and anxious injunctions swing between what is broad and what is creative. A visitor from outer space would conclude that we had lost, or perhaps never formed, any communicable idea of the purpose of schools.

We did have such an idea until about 1900, when it began to yield to the indefiniteness of mass education. But that phrase alone is enough to quell our impatience. We can never forget the magnitude of the difficulties in what we then undertook. The worst faults of the schooling we now give are due to the large numbers of pupils relative to the natural supply of true teachers. And most of the other faults are due to the unending task of acclimating the alien and native millions to increasingly complicated modes of life. If the high schools make dating and "driver education" part of the curriculum in place of Latin and trigonometry, it is because "preparing for life" means giving information that is of everyday use, fraught with social consequence, and that no one else will impart.[5]

[2] William H. Kilpatrick, Professor Emeritus of Education in Teachers College.

[3] William H. Kilpatrick, "How Should Teachers Be Educated?" *The Educational Forum*, March, 1956, 287-91.

[4] Edward L. Bernays, "Public Relations for Higher Education," an Address to the American College Public Relations Association, Omaha, June 24, 1957, 5 and ff.

[5] I have paid my sincere respects to the principle of "preparation for life," and to the teachers who carry it out, in an essay entitled "The Battle Over Brains in Democratic Education" (*University of Toronto Quarterly*, January, 1954). In the present chapter I take the point for granted and go on to discuss our schooling in its relation to Intellect.

But what of Intellect and its ancient nursery, the classical curriculum? The answer is soon given. Who would teach it? How many parents would approve of it? How would children respond to it? Suppose it magically restored, what gaps and failures in the common mind would immediately be deplored, unrelieved by scattered intellectual accomplishments that millions of citizens would rightly deem useless?

It is a proof of the low state of our Intellect that the present debate on education refers to "our schools" at large, without marking off kinds and grades. People argue for "more science" or "the liberal arts" or "better English" or "a longer siege of American history," without considering the conditions of teaching and study that now obtain. Nor is due attention given to the country's beliefs and acts regarding Intellect and its employment. No doubt the continual comparisons with "Soviet education," of which very few know anything reliable, have upset us; and so has the image of the "tidal wave" of youth expected by 1970. This prospect in turn leads to agitation about the educational use of television and other machinery, again in the belief that multiplying voices, rooms, and seats to the right number will bring "education" to the newcomers. Whether the educating that now goes on face to face will remain the same when put on the screen is a question seldom raised. Hardly anyone knows what does go on, nor is there agreement about what should go on and does not.

The confusion is not ours alone. Most of Europe is recasting its old systems, also in the dark. According to one survey, some forty nations of the world are short of teachers and engaged in school reform. Considering how dreary educational discussion is, the number of people now being bored with it must exceed any previous maximum. What is especially distressing is that our own brand of theory and practice is now reaching to the antipodes and threatening to eclipse there the demands of Intellect. From Tasmania, for instance, comes an official pamphlet entitled "Learning Is Living," which details the island's adult education program. The title by itself reveals what a congenial error overtakes modern states on the threshold of mass education.

It is the error of supposing that because under popular government all good things are for everybody, it follows that all things whatever are interfused and all distinctions are false. This is the belief that we saw at work in journalism and publishing, and again in democratic manners. If it is indeed true that "learning is living," then the school loses its institutional—its properly artificial—character, and soon people forget that learning requires attention and assiduity. They end by repudiating the school and entrust to some sort of pseudo-schooling, some "life-like" contrivance, the task of teaching.

Yes, but what is wrong with life? Do we not say: "experience teaches, suffering educates"? That is just the trouble. We do, and we mean, or should mean, something indefinite, quite remote from schooling. Meanwhile the strange pantheism which finds learning and living identical comes from these shores: "I learn what I live," says Dr. Kilpatrick,[6] "and I learn it as I accept it . . . I learn it in the degree that I live it . . . I learn what I live. What is learned is the inner object of the verb to live. We learn the content of our living and learn this content as we accept consciously to live it." This incantation is powerful—the seat of learning is the liver.

The fallacy is buried in the damnable word "education," from which all this wordplay started, and which we now find emblazoned in all the mansions of life. Besides all the educating for health, character, happiness, and pedestrian safety, we now have driver education and alcohol education,[7] cancer education and sex education—just as next to the *Education of Henry Adams* we have *The Education of a Poker Player*.[8] The advertisers educate us to the fact that a new detergent is afloat and an old oil company has changed its name.[9] A thousand and one leagues have "campaigns of education," which means occupying space in the papers and teaching us by correspondence their pressing need of cash. The YMCAs and evening schools, the Sunrise Semesters and Midnight Colleges[10] all profess to educate "in" something—business English or the Australian crawl: never was so much sharing of crafts and powers carried on with such good will and so little uneasiness of mind.

The word "education" should accordingly be reserved for all this, which it has conquered, and absolutely banned from discussions of *schooling* and *instruction*, which in an evil day it replaced.[11] "Education"

---

[6] W. H. Kilpatrick, *loc. cit.*

[7] Cf. the handbook by Joseph Hirsch.

[8] By the late Herbert O. Yardley, the distinguished cryptologist and poker player.

[9] See the report on the Calso "educational campaign" to implant the "complicated idea" that its name has changed. *New York Times*, May 23, 1958.

[10] Sunrise Semester, the first television course offered for credit, by New York University; Midnight College, a comparable undertaking by Fairleigh Dickinson College in New Jersey; Continental Classroom, a national and co-operative form of the same.

[11] When the French schools became less competitive and took on more welfare

sounds "broad," a richer, more philanthropic gift than "instruction." There is less of superior-to-inferior in it, hence egalitarian manners prefer it—we are all educating ourselves together; and—cheerful thought! —education is never done, whereas in instruction there is a point (or should be) at which one knows how to read, count, write, speak German, and understand physics. Education also suggests—rightly so—the diversity of men's minds and talents, which seek different ends; it is thus the more democratic and liberal word. The modern vision of endless creativity, the love of art and the relish for indefinite inwardness also call for "education," the all-inclusive. Finally, science in the form of psychology and "guidance" has transformed teaching and learning into "the educational process" and made teaching and instruction seem dry and mean. Educate, educator, educationist—the names permit a humble profession, armed with method, to permeate our life with its confident pretensions.

These things being so, we must, if we really intend to change our schools, forget the language, and especially the slogans, of mass education. They betray the user as well as the listener. "Keeping the schools democratic," preventing them from "producing an elite," insisting on "giving all our children the same education" would not satisfy the very people who fight for these "principles," if "education" were omitted and the other words replaced by honestly descriptive ones: shall all children receive *instruction* in the same subjects through high school, whether they or their parents want the same or not? We say we need research scientists and engineers: does the choice of these careers require different instruction from hotel-keeping and shorthand and typewriting, or does it not? Does training a group of scientists at public expense in high schools and state universities create an elite likely to lord it over hotel managers and stenographers? Or more generally, does social equality depend on the possession of identical knowledge? This question of different training clearly applies as well to scholars in the humanities and the social sciences (who, it seems, are also wanted men) and to lawyers, doctors, accountants, and other professionals.

As for keeping the schools "democratic" in the sense of ignoring differences of ability and "giving" a college career to all who ask for it, this is the scheme which has just broken down and brought many people to the realization that it is wasteful, dangerous, and unjust.

---

activities in the mid-1920's, the Ministry of Public Instruction turned into the Ministry of National Education—the change is a description in itself.

Ability and achievement are too important to the country to be any longer trifled with, as has been done by maintaining that failure is something a child must invariably be shielded from, lest he take a dislike to learning.[12] True, every reproof must be accompanied by encouragement, and error should not be represented to youth as irrevocable. But none of this means that to fail is one way of succeeding. The analogy of athletics must be pressed until all recognize that in the exertions of Intellect those who lack the muscles, co-ordination, and will power can claim no place at the training table, let alone on the playing field.

Why did we ever think otherwise? Part of the answer has been given in earlier chapters dealing with democratic manners and opinion, but there is so far something peculiarly American about the institution of the child-centered school. Americans began by loving youth, and now, out of adult self-pity they worship it. At the same time, in all their institutions, they do not merely desire, but work for the widest sociability. The American atmosphere requires that everybody present shall participate, have a good time, share the good things, and help maintain the universal good-fellowship. This outlook may recall by inherited memory the brotherhood of the humble transplanted from Europe, or it may spring from the more bourgeois doctrine of equality. However it may be, in such a moral climate it was inevitable that our schools should aim at social adjustment first, even if practical needs had not made this convenient. On the one hand, "adjustment" helps to assimilate the foreigner and the poor; on the other, it respects the resistance of the majority to intellectual work and makes teachers of many with no special talents.[13]

When, therefore, critics from the universities attack our public schools for anti-intellectualism, on the assumption that it would take only a high resolve and a changed curriculum to make them seminaries of Intellect, the attack falls harmlessly against the solid barrier of facts:

---

[12] To quote Dr. Kilpatrick again: "Suppose a teacher scolds a boy for failure at fractions. That boy may next time study harder as the teacher hoped and intended. But the boy is likely to react inwardly against the scolding with some feelings against the teacher, and against some other boys who snickered at his scolding, and against fractions, and arithmetic, and school. Also he may be feeling that he is a comparative failure. . . . The older education seldom took account of such learnings except as it tried by advice and reproof to build them into the young." *Op. cit.*, 289.

[13] An English observer of his country's social revolution ascribes to working-class tolerance the entire absence of standards. See *The Uses of Literacy*, by Richard Hoggart, London, 1957.

we cannot make intellectuals out of two million pupils—too many are incapable of the effort even a modestly bookish education requires; too many have the good sense to know that they want instead some vocational training that will be immediately marketable.[14]

The only answer is the selection and special schooling of those with a talent for abstraction, articulateness, and the pursuit of ideas in books. This selection need not mean a new kind of segregation; many classes can be shared by all the children in a school, special classes will speed the intellectually strong toward their goals. Recent attempts to "adjust" in this new way have proved to school authorities that the heavens do not fall at this differentiation and—what they feared even more than divine wrath—that parents do not protest, but accept philosophically the accident of brains. It seems as if after sixty years of rugged trial American education were making its way out of the lowlands. We could be cheerful about this if it were not for two handicaps: the coming "tidal wave," which will strain school funds and obscure recent gains, and the almost total lack of intellectual attachments among those who think they lead our schools.

---

[14]I agree with Mr. Conant and disagree with Mr. Mortimer Adler about the latter's intention to provide the liberal arts for all. (See Mr. Adler's articles in the Chicago *Sun-Times* for January 19, 1958.) For sidelights from the German scene, see the articles by Helmut Becker on the need for a new education in *Das Parlament,* 3:January 22, 1958, 5; and by Helmut Schelsky on vocational training in *Die Zeit,* October, 1957, Feuilleton page.

ARTHUR E. BESTOR

Arthur E. Bestor was born at Chautauqua, New York, on September 20, 1908. He attended the progressively oriented Lincoln High School of Teachers College, Columbia University, and graduated in 1926. He then entered Yale where he majored in English. He received a Ph.B. degree in 1930, and in 1938 a Ph.D. in history.

Bestor's father, Arthur Eugene Bestor, had been the president of the Chautauqua Institution for 30 years, and Arthur E. Bestor, Jr., served as the editor-in-chief of the *Chautauqua Daily* from 1931 to 1933.

Bestor has taught at Yale University, Teachers College, Columbia University, Stanford University, University of Wisconsin, University of Illinois, Oxford University, and the University of Washington.

Bestor has long been concerned with American education and has written a number of books about education including *The Restoration of Learning: A Program for Redeeming the Unfulfilled Promise of American Education,* and *Educational Wastelands: The Retreat from Learning in Our Public Schools.*

In 1956 Bestor became the first president of The Council for Basic Education which was established as a way of promoting more basic education courses in the curriculums of our elementary and high schools. Since 1956 over 10 scientific and learned societies have become affiliated with the council.

Bestor has often been referred to as a "gadfly" of American education, and he has achieved notoriety for his opposition to "frills" in place of sound academic programs in our schools. Bestor has been outspoken in his criticism of Progressivism and "professional educators." He has been praised as a crusader, and damned as a troublemaker. He believes that at the present time our schools seriously lack any direction, and that the goal of all education should be the development of man's intellectual powers.

EDUCATIONAL WASTELANDS

Arthur E. Bestor

Americans have unbounded faith in schools, but they seem to distrust the results of schooling. We send, at public expense, an ever-increasing proportion of the population to school and college, yet we are suspicious of the highly educated man who offers to make some return by devoting his special training to the public service. At graduation we are proud to see our sons and daughters march forward in cap and gown, but in the morning newspaper we recognize the very same cap and gown as the cartoonist's accepted symbol for folly and ineffectiveness.

Universal, free, public education is part of the democratic creed, which Americans accept but which they would find it hard to explain in rational terms. It does not appear that many of them seriously expect society to get its money's worth out of the process. We pay our school taxes, but we rarely conceive of ourselves as making thereby an investment in the intellectual advancement of the nation. Our motive seems to be little more than warm-hearted benevolence. We hate to think that any child should be deprived of his fair share of anything so costly, so ornamental, and so well-regarded as education. To put the matter bluntly, we regard schooling as a mere experience, delightful to the recipient but hardly valuable to society. The school or college has become, to our minds, merely a branch of the luxury-purveying trade. Like the club car on a passenger train, it dispenses the amenities of life to persons bound on serious errands elsewhere.

Now, public opinion is not so perverse as to adopt such a view

Arthur E. Bestor. *Educational Wastelands*, The University of Illinois Press, Urbana, 1953, pp. 1-11. © 1953 by The University of Illinois Press and reprinted by permission.

without cause. It is fully aware of the traditional claims of education. It is prepared to believe that knowledge is a good thing both in its own right and for the practical uses to which it can be put. It sees a connection between good citizenship and the ability to think. What it is skeptical about is the ability of our schools and colleges to impart these qualities of mind to their graduates. Responsibility for this disbelief rests squarely upon the men and women who are professionally engaged in education. They have allowed themselves to become confused about the purposes of education, and they have transmitted that confusion to the public. They have sponsored school and college programs which make no substantial contribution to knowledge or to clear thinking, and which could not conceivably make such a contribution. The public, seeing no point in much of what is done under the name of education, have developed a justifiable skepticism toward education itself. They are willing to keep on playing the game, but they refuse to think of it as much more than a game.

The founders of our nation and of our school system betrayed no such confusion of purpose. "If a nation expects to be ignorant and free," wrote Thomas Jefferson, ". . . it expects what never was and never will be." Jefferson intended his words to be taken literally. He knew, moreover, what he meant by education. It is, first of all, the opposite of ignorance. Its positive meaning is indicated by the synonyms which Jefferson employs in his letters. The kind of schooling that is vital to a democratic society is the kind that results in the "spread of information" and the "diffusion of knowledge"; the kind that regards "science . . . [as] more important in a republican than in any other government"; the kind that recognizes that "the general mind must be strengthened by education"; the kind that aims to make the people "enlightened" and to "inform their discretion." These are the ends which the schools must serve if a free people is to remain free. These, be it noted, are intellectual ends. Genuine education, in short, is intellectual training.

The founders of our public school system meant by education exactly what Jefferson meant by education and exactly what thoughtful men had always meant by it. They believed, quite simply, that ignorance is a handicap and disciplined intelligence a source of power. A democracy, they argued, should make intellectual training available to every citizen, whether poor or rich. So great would be the benefit to the state from such a diffusion of knowledge and intelligence that it was legitimate to support the educational system by taxation, and even to use the coercive authority of law to compel every future citizen to secure an education by attending school for a substantial period of time.

The American people, more than a century ago, committed themselves to this program, and they have invested heavily in the effort to bring it to full realization. By every quantitative measure—time, effort, numbers, money—we should be well on the way toward achievement of the noble ends in view. Enrollment has steadily increased until today four out of every five American children between the ages of five and seventeen, inclusive, are in school. We talk so much about overcrowding that we are apt to forget the significant fact that the equipment and resources of the public schools have increased far more rapidly than attendance. Approximately four times as many children as in 1870 are now in school, but we spend more than ninety times as much on their education. The child of today enjoys a school year twice as long. The proportion of teachers to pupils is greater, and the teachers are required to have spent far more time in training. Compared with 1870 (*after* adjustments have been made for the changed value of the dollar), we find that nine times as much money is spent per year on the education of *each* child, and nearly thirteen times as much is invested in the buildings and equipment which each one is privileged to use. Inequalities and inadequacies persist, of course, and these must be eliminated. But the fact remains that the American people have generously and faithfully supported their schools. They have a right to ask whether the qualitative educational achievement of our public schools is commensurate with the money and effort that have been invested in them. In effect this is to ask whether school administrators have been as faithful to the ideal of democratic education as have the American people.

Admittedly it is a complicated task to measure the effectiveness of a school system. But on almost every count there is general dissatisfaction with the results of the twelve years of education currently provided by most of our public schools. And it is an exceedingly important fact that the criticisms come with greatest intensity from those who believe most strongly in the value and importance of education, and who, by their professions, are best qualified to judge what sound education consists in. Discontent with the training which the public schools provide is all but unanimous, I discover, among members of the liberal arts and professional faculties of our universities and colleges. It is almost equally widespread among doctors, engineers, clergymen, lawyers, and other professional men throughout the nation. Business men are dismayed at the deficiencies

25

in reading, writing, arithmetic, and general knowledge displayed by the high school and college graduates they employ. Parents are alarmed at the educational handicaps under which their children are obliged to labor as they enter upon the serious business of life.

In every community, searching questions about present-day educational policy are being raised by intelligent, responsible, disinterested citizens. The criticism is not that of "reactionaries." Among my acquaintances and correspondents, the liberals in political and social matters are just as outspoken in their denunciation of current trends in the public schools as are the men and women whose views can be labelled conservative. Upon college and university faculties the criticism does not come primarily from classicists in the older "traditional" branches of learning; it comes with perhaps greatest intensity from professors in the sciences, in mathematics, and in the other disciplines directly connected with the problems of a modern technological world.

The defense of their stewardship that is offered by public school administrators and by their allies in university departments of education is so feeble as to amount to a confession of failure. They quote criticisms of earlier date to show that discontent in the past was as great as it is today. The logic is that of Looking-Glass Land, where, the Red Queen explained to Alice, "it takes all the running you can do, to keep in the same place. If you want to get somewhere else, you must run at least twice as fast as that!" In every other area of American life progress is measured in terms of defects overcome. Only the professional educationists take pride in the fact that, though they run several times as hard, they can always be found by their critics in pretty much the same spot.

Some improvement, indeed, the professional educationists do claim, but the evidence they adduce is exceedingly slight and scattered, and it never gives weight to the vastly increased time, effort, and money which have gone into producing the results described. Typical of the evidence which school administrators offer is this: "Arithmetic tests given to ninth-grade pupils in Springfield, Massachusetts, in 1845, were administered to Minneapolis eighth-graders in 1926. The percent of correct answers in 1845 was 29.4 as compared to 67.1 in 1926." If these figures could be accepted as a valid statistical sample, they would merely prove that when the elementary schools stick to their traditional tasks they do a job appreciably better than the ill-equipped and financially impoverished schools of a century ago, with their short school terms and their inadequately trained teachers. In weighing this evidence let us remember (as a previous paragraph has pointed out) that by the time a pupil has finished a given grade today, he will have spent twice as many days in school as a comparable student would have spent eighty years ago. He will have received a greater share of the personal attention of a better trained teacher. Nine times as much money will have been expended in his education, and he will have used buildings and equipment at least thirteen times as good. A comparison with 1845, could it be made, would show an even greater increase in resources. If the achievement of a present-day student is only a little greater than that of his predecessor, instead of several times as great, there has been an alarming decline in the efficiency of public school instruction.

To choose such a standard of comparison in the first place is evidence that professional educationists have all but forgotten the high aims and ideals of American public education. We did not set out to make a fourth-rate educational system into a third-rate one. We have invested more money in education than any other nation because we want the best education for our children that money can buy. No serious critic of modern American education is asserting that the public schools enjoyed a golden age in the past. It is the shortcomings of the schools today that concern us. If we are to have improvement, we must learn to make comparisons, not with the wretchedly inadequate public schools of earlier generations, but with the very best schools, public or private, American or foreign, past or present, of which we can obtain any knowledge. The failure of virtually all professional educationists to make such comparisons is one of their gravest derelictions of duty. Their measuring-rod seems always to be what poor schools used to do, never what good schools have done, can do, and ought to do.

The present effectiveness of the schools, measured against the best that can possibly be achieved, is the only valid measure of our educational accomplishment. If some other nation designs a better military plane, our aeronautical engineers do not point smugly to the fact that our own aircraft are better than they were in 1920 or 1930 or 1940. They accept the challenge of equalling or bettering the best that any other nation can produce. We would take them grimly to task if they adopted any lesser aim, for we are realistic enough in these matters to know that a lesser aim would be no aim at all but an invitation to national disaster. If we take education seriously, we can no more afford to gamble our safety upon inferior intellectual training in our schools than upon inferior weapons in our armory.

If we propose to make American schools the world's finest, we cannot avoid studying, and perhaps borrowing from, the best educational systems of other places and times. We must demand that our schools be superior to the less adequately financed educational systems of other countries—superior in the intellectual discipline which they provide in languages, history, mathematics, and science. We must welcome comparisons between the graduates of our public schools and the graduates of the best private schools of the present and the past. If we cannot equal the achievement of these other schools, then we should know why. If it is lack of money, then the people should be realistically informed of the cost of giving all our children the truly best in education. If, as I suspect, it is a difference in method or aim, then we should adopt as a guide in these matters, not the methods and aims that present-day educationists have spun out of their own heads, but the methods and aims that have proved themselves in the practice of the best educational systems of the world.

We must, moreover, measure the achievement of our schools against an even more rigorous standard. Are they giving to the people and to the nation the values which were the promised result of universal public education? If the schools are doing their job, we should expect educators to point to a significant and indisputable achievement in raising the intellectual level of the nation—measured perhaps by larger per capita circulation of books and serious magazines, by definitely improved taste in movies and radio programs, by higher standards of political debate, by increased respect for freedom of speech and of thought, by a marked decline in such evidences of mental retardation as the incessant reading of comic books by adults. We should expect superintendents to report that because of improved methods of instruction, longer school years, and better trained teachers they have been able to teach successfully in the high school many of the fundamental disciplines to which students were formerly introduced only in college. We should expect school administrators to produce testimonials from employers, professional men, college professors, and officers of the armed services to the effect that young men and women are coming out of high school with sounder intellectual background and greater skill and competence than ever before.

No such claims are being advanced and no such comparisons are being made by the men and women to whom we have entrusted the control of our public schools. They do not ask that the American public schools be judged by such standards. They do not ask it, because, by and large, they no longer accept these as valid standards. There are many honorable exceptions, of course, but the most influential men in the field of elementary and secondary education have, for a generation, been redefining the purposes of the public schools in a fashion that amounts to a repudiation of these objectives. The charge which this book advances is that professional educationists, in their policy-making role, have lowered the aims of the American public schools. And because the sights have been lowered, no possible increase in pedagogical efficiency can ever enable our schools as currently administered to reach the target which the American people originally set up for them.

In the last analysis, it is not lack of effort but lack of direction that has resulted in the mediocre showing of our public high schools. Where educational aims have been well conceived, as in many fields of higher education and professional training, the money and the effort that Americans have poured into education have produced unmistakable progress. Seventy-five years ago American public schools were poor, but so too was American training for medicine, for law, and for research in the sciences and arts. All these fields have shared in the great American effort for educational improvement. But how different are the results! Would we be satisfied to hear the dean of a medical school assert merely that doctors today are just as well prepared as when they learned the theory of medicine in a few months of lectures and picked up the practice in the back office of an old-fashioned sawbones?

The difference is not a matter of money. It is a matter of adequate aims. In the sciences, in scholarship, in the learned professions, the men responsible for educational progress have been scholars and scientists in their own right. They have begun by accepting the traditional aims of their respective disciplines and professions, and they have defined their task as the carrying out of these recognized aims in a manner more effective than ever before. They have deliberately measured their achievement, not in terms of some slight improvement over the past, but in terms of the best that could possibly be done by any man, in any place, at any time. Until public school educationists can learn to think in this same way—until they acquire sufficient intellectual humility to accept the guidance of past experience and of the considered judgment of the modern learned world—no amount of financial support can possibly raise our schools above mediocrity. And mediocrity, given the possibilities which

America offers to public education, is nothing else than downright failure.

Since I am critical of current practices in American education, I shall be automatically branded an enemy of the public schools by those who have a vested interest in the educational status quo. This charge has been used before by educational administrators to silence criticism, and it will be used again. It is a curiously perverse argument, which belongs to dictatorship, not to democracy. When the citizen of a free state criticizes the policies of a political party in office, he is not attacking government itself. When he denounces a bureaucrat as incompetent, he is not saying that the work of the bureau ought not to be done and done well. In point of fact, he is reaffirming his faith in an institution every time he insists upon holding its responsible managers to strict accountability. In the same manner, he is reaffirming his faith in public education whenever he insists that it *be* education and not something else. We are fools if we allow a politician to tell us that we cannot attack him without undermining government. We are no less fools if we permit professional educationists to tell us that we cannot criticize their policies without becoming enemies of the public schools.

To dispel any doubts about my position, however, let me offer at the outset a full and frank confession of faith. I am a firm believer in the principle of universal, public, democratic education. As a professor in a state university I am part of an institution dedicated to that very principle, and I am proud to be so. I believe that publicly financed education from the nursery school through the highest levels of graduate and professional instruction is essential to American democracy as we know and value it. I have no sympathy whatever with anyone who proposes to cut school appropriations in such a way as to limit educational opportunity or impair the quality of instruction. That is the road not to reform but to ruin. I believe in doing away with every barrier that race, religion, or economic status interposes to prevent any American from pursuing to the highest levels any form of study for which he has the intellectual capacity, the desire, and the will.

I believe that the United States is wealthy enough to afford the best education for its future citizens. I believe, moreover, that the American people are ready to pay the price, if only they are assured that what they are buying is genuinely good public education. One of the gravest charges that can be made against the professional educationists is that they have undermined public confidence in the schools by setting forth purposes

fantastic !

for education so trivial as to forfeit the respect of thoughtful men, and by deliberately divorcing the schools from the disciplines of science and scholarship, which citizens trust and value. The treasure of public confidence that the educationists have frittered away can be garnered again, I am convinced, once the public schools set for themselves goals that are worthy of such confidence.

I believe, finally, in academic freedom. I conceive it to be the scholar's duty to resist every effort to stifle the free and responsible investigation and discussion of public issues. And I stand ready to oppose to the uttermost any group that seeks to limit or pervert the curricula of schools and colleges so as to impose upon them its own narrow and dogmatic preconceptions concerning matters that are properly the subject of free and objective inquiry.

These are not merely my personal convictions. They are, it seems to me, part and parcel of the ideal of liberal education which I am defending. It is because liberal education is synonymous with intellectual freedom that it needs to be constantly defended. And part of my criticism of professional educationists is that they, by misrepresenting and undervaluing liberal education, have contributed—unwillingly perhaps, but nevertheless effectually—to the growth of an anti-intellectualist hysteria that threatens not merely the schools but freedom itself.

I trust that my position is clear. I stand for an American public school system that shall be free and democratic. I stand also for an American public school system that shall be *educational*. There is an antique play on words that still seems to tickle the fancy of professional educationists. "We do not teach history," they say, "we teach children." The implication that those who teach history teach it to no one is a manifest impossibility, no classrooms being located in the empty desert. But it *is* a distinct possibility, alas, that educationists, following their own maxim, may succeed in teaching children—*nothing*.

The thesis of this book is that schools exist to teach *something*, and that this something is the power to think. To assert this, of course, is to assert the importance of good teaching. Professional educationists are fond of beclouding the issue by suggesting that those who believe in disciplined intellectual training deny the importance of good teaching. Nothing could be farther from the truth. It is sheer presumption on their part to pose as the only persons in the academic world with a concern for good teaching. Disciplined intellectual training depends on good teaching, and scholars and scientists in American universities have shown as much genuine concern with good teaching as professors of education, many of whom betray an amazing disregard of its principles in the conduct of their own classes.

The issue in American education today is not drawn between those who believe in scholarship but are indifferent to good teaching, and those who believe in good teaching but are indifferent to scholarship. The issue is drawn between those who believe that good teaching should be directed to sound intellectual ends, and those who are content to dethrone intellectual values and cultivate the techniques of teaching for their own sake, in an intellectual and cultural vacuum.

JEROME S. BRUNER

Jerome S. Bruner was born on October 1, 1915, in New York City. He received a B.A. from Duke University in psychology in 1937, and his M.A. and Ph.D. from Harvard University in 1939 and 1941 respectively.

In 1942 he became Associate Director of Public Opinion Research at Princeton, and from 1943 to the end of World War II he served abroad with the French in political intelligence. In 1945 he returned to Harvard where he taught educational psychology. In 1955 he received a Guggenheim fellowship from Cambridge University and later a fellowship from the American Psychology Association. He served on a White House panel on educational research and development during the Eisenhower administration, and was appointed education advisor for the book division of Time, Inc. In 1959 he served as chairman of the Woods Hole Conference sponsored by the National Academy of Science, and he has been Director of the Center for Cognitive Studies at Harvard since 1961. In 1962 he received the award for Distinguished Science Contribution from the National Academy of Science, and in 1965 he was appointed a Bacon professor at the University of Aix-en-Provence in France.

Bruner has written a number of books about education, such as *The Process of Education* and *Toward a Theory of Instruction.*

Bruner disagrees with those educators who believe that a child is only ready for certain subjects later in his schooling, and believes that any subject can be taught effectively in some intellectually honest form to any child at any stage of development. He feels that a child should be helped to discover things for himself, and believes that a good curriculum stresses structure rather than details. Too much of modern education, Bruner feels, is learning without understanding.

THE PROCESS OF EDUCATION

Jerome S. Bruner

The first object of any act of learning, over and beyond the pleasure it may give, is that it should serve us in the future. Learning should not only take us somewhere; it should allow us later to go further more easily. There are two ways in which learning serves the future. One is through its specific applicability to tasks that are highly similar to those we originally learned to perform. Psychologists refer to this phenomenon as specific transfer of training; perhaps it should be called the extension of habits or associations. Its utility appears to be limited in the main to what we usually speak of as skills. Having learned how to hammer nails, we are better able later to learn how to hammer tacks or chip wood. Learning in school undoubtedly creates skills of a kind that transfers to activities encountered later, either in school or after. A second way in which earlier learning renders later performance more efficient is through what is conveniently called nonspecific transfer, or, more accurately, the transfer of principles and attitudes. In essence, it consists of learning initially not a skill but a general idea, which can then be used as a basis for recognizing subsequent problems as special cases of the idea originally mastered. This type of transfer is at the heart of the educational process—the continual broadening and deepening of knowledge in terms of basic and general ideas.

The continuity of learning that is produced by the second type of transfer, transfer of principles, is dependent upon mastery of the structure of the subject matter. That is to say, in order for a person to be able to recognize the applicability or inapplicability of an idea to a new

Jerome S. Bruner. *The Process of Education*, Vintage Books, New York, 1960, pp. 17-20, 33-40. © 1960 by Jerome S. Bruner and reprinted by permission.

situation and to broaden his learning thereby, he must have clearly in mind the general nature of the phenomenon with which he is dealing. The more fundamental or basic is the idea he has learned, almost by definition, the greater will be its breadth of applicability to new problems. Indeed, this is almost a tautology, for what is meant by "fundamental" in this sense is precisely that an idea has wide as well as powerful applicability. It is simple enough to proclaim, of course, that school curricula and methods of teaching should be geared to the teaching of fundamental ideas in whatever subject is being taught. But as soon as one makes such a statement a host of problems arise, many of which can be solved only with the aid of considerably more research. We turn to some of these now.

The first and most obvious problem is how to construct curricula that can be taught by ordinary teachers to ordinary students and that at the same time reflect clearly the basic or underlying principles of various fields of inquiry. The problem is twofold: first, how to have the basic subjects rewritten and their teaching materials revamped in such a way that the pervading and powerful ideas and attitudes relating to them are given a central role; second, how to match the levels of these materials to the capacities of students of different abilities at different grades in school.

The experience of the past several years has taught at least one important lesson about the design of a curriculum that is true to the underlying structure of its subject matter. It is that the best minds in any particular discipline must be put to work on the task. The decision as to what should be taught in American history to elementary school children or what should be taught in arithmetic is a decision that can best be reached with the aid of those with a high degree of vision and competence in each of these fields. To decide that the elementary ideas of algebra depend upon the fundamentals of the commutative, distributive, and associative laws, one must be a mathematician in a position to appreciate and understand the fundamentals of mathematics. Whether school children require an understanding of Frederick Jackson Turner's ideas about the role of the frontier in American history before they can sort out the facts and trends of American history—this again is a decision that requires the help of the scholar who has a deep understanding of the American past. Only by the use of our best minds in devising curricula will we bring the fruits of scholarship and wisdom to the student just beginning his studies.

The question will be raised, "How enlist the aid of our most able scholars and scientists in designing curricula for primary and secondary schools?" The answer has already been given, at least in part. The School Mathematics Study Group, the University of Illinois mathematics projects, the Physical Science Study Committee, and the Biological Sciences Curriculum Study have indeed been enlisting the aid of eminent men in their various fields, doing so by means of summer projects, supplemented in part by year-long leaves of absence for certain key people involved. They have been aided in the projects by outstanding elementary and secondary school teachers and, for special purposes, by professional writers, film makers, designers, and others required in such a complex enterprise.

There is at least one major matter that is left unsettled even by a large-scale revision of curricula in the direction indicated. Mastery of the fundamental ideas of a field involves not only the grasping of general principles, but also the development of an attitude toward learning and inquiry, toward the possibility of solving problems on one's own. Just as a physicist has certain attitudes about the ultimate orderliness of nature and a conviction that order can be discovered, so a young physics student needs some working version of these attitudes if he is to organize his learning in such a way as to make what he learns usable and meaningful in his thinking. To instill such attitudes by teaching requires something more than the mere presentation of fundamental ideas. Just what it takes to bring off such teaching is something on which a great deal of research is needed, but it would seem that an important ingredient is a sense of excitement about discovery—discovery of regularities of previously unrecognized relations and similarities between ideas, with a resulting sense of self-confidence in one's abilities. Various people who have worked on curricula in science and mathematics have urged that it is possible to present the fundamental structure of a discipline in such a way as to preserve some of the exciting sequences that lead a student to discover for himself.

*　　*　　*

We begin with the hypothesis that any subject can be taught effectively in some intellectually honest form to any child at any stage of development. It is a bold hypothesis and an essential one in thinking about the nature of a curriculum. No evidence exists to contradict it; considerable evidence is being amassed that supports it.

To make clear what is implied, let us examine three general ideas. The first has to do with the process of intellectual development in children, the second with the act of learning, and the third with the notion of the "spiral curriculum."

Intellectual development. Research on the intellectual development of the child highlights the fact that at each stage of development the child has a characteristic way of viewing the world and explaining it to himself. The task of teaching a subject to a child at any particular age is one of representing the structure of that subject in terms of the child's way of viewing things. The general hypothesis that has just been stated is premised on the considered judgment that any idea can be represented honestly and usefully in the thought forms of children of school age, and that these first representations can later be made more powerful and precise the more easily by virtue of his early learning. To illustrate and support this view, we present here a somewhat detailed picture of the course of intellectual development, along with some suggestions about teaching at different stages of it.

The work of Piaget and others suggests that, roughly speaking, one may distinguish three stages in the intellectual development of the child. The first stage need not concern us in detail, for it is characteristic principally of the pre-school child. In this stage, which ends (at least for Swiss school children) around the fifth or sixth year, the child's mental work consists principally in establishing relationships between experience and action; his concern is with manipulating the world through action. This stage corresponds roughly to the period from the first development of language to the point at which the child learns to manipulate symbols. In this so-called preoperational stage, the principal symbolic achievement is that the child learns how to represent the external world through symbols established by simple generalization; things are represented as equivalent in terms of sharing some common property. But the child's symbolic world does not make a clear separation between internal motives and feelings on the one hand and external reality on the other. The sun moves because God pushes it, and the stars, like himself, have to go to bed. The child is little able to separate his own goals from the means for achieving them, and when he has to make corrections in his activity after unsuccessful attempts at manipulating reality, he does so by what are called intuitive regulations rather than by symbolic operation, the former being of a crude trial-and-error nature rather than the result of taking thought.

What is principally lacking at this stage of development is what the

Geneva school has called the concept of reversibility. When the shape of an object is changed, as when one changes the shape of a ball of plasticene, the preoperational child cannot grasp the idea that it can be brought back readily to its original state. Because of this fundamental lack the child cannot understand certain fundamental ideas that lie at the basis of mathematics and physics—the mathematical idea that one conserves quantity even when one partitions a set of things into subgroups, or the physical idea that one conserves mass and weight even though one transforms the shape of an object. It goes without saying that teachers are severely limited in transmitting concepts to a child at this stage, even in a highly intuitive manner.

The second stage of development—and now the child is in school—is called the stage of concrete operations. This stage is operational in contrast to the preceding stage, which is merely active. An operation is a type of action: it can be carried out rather directly by the manipulation of objects, or internally, as when one manipulates the symbols that represent things and relations in one's mind. Roughly, an operation is a means of getting data about the real world into the mind and there transforming them so that they can be organized and used selectively in the solution of problems. Assume a child is presented with a pinball machine which bounces a ball off a wall at an angle. Let us find out what he appreciates about the relation between the angle of incidence and the angle of reflection. The young child sees no problem; for him, the ball travels in an arc, touching the wall on the way. The somewhat older child, say age ten, sees the two angles as roughly related—as one changes so does the other. The still older child begins to grasp that there is a fixed relation between the two, and usually says it is a right angle. Finally, the thirteen- or fourteen-year-old, often by pointing the ejector directly at the wall and seeing the ball come back at the ejector, gets the idea that the two angles are equal. Each way of looking at the phenomenon represents the result of an operation in this sense, and the child's thinking is constrained by his way of pulling his observations together.

An operation differs from simple action or goal-directed behavior in that it is internalized and reversible. "Internalized" means that the child does not have to go about his problem-solving any longer by overt trial and error, but can actually carry out trial and error in his head. Reversibility is present because operations are seen as characterized where appropriate by what is called "complete compensation"; that is to say, an operation can be compensated for by an inverse operation. If marbles, for example, are divided into subgroups, the child can grasp intuitively that the original collection of marbles can be restored by being added back together again. The child tips a balance scale too far with a weight and then searches systematically for a lighter weight or for something with which to get the scale rebalanced. He may carry reversibility too far by assuming that a piece of paper, once burned, can also be restored.

With the advent of concrete operations, the child develops an internalized structure with which to operate. In the example of the balance scale, the structure is a serial order of weights that the child has in his mind. Such internal structures are of the essence. They are the internalized symbolic systems by which the child represents the world, as in the example of the pinball machine and the angles of incidence and reflection. It is into the language of these internal structures that one must translate ideas if the child is to grasp them.

But concrete operations, though they are guided by the logic of classes and the logic of relations, are means for structuring only immediately present reality. The child is able to give structure to the things he encounters, but he is not yet readily able to deal with possibilities not directly before him or not already experienced. This is not to say that children operating concretely are not able to anticipate things that are not present. Rather, it is that they do not command the operations for conjuring up systematically the full range of alternative possibilities that could exist at any given time. They cannot go systematically beyond the information given them to a description of what else might occur. Somewhere between ten and fourteen years of age the child passes into a third stage, which is called the stage of "formal operations" by the Geneva school.

Now the child's intellectual activity seems to be based upon an ability to operate on hypothetical propositions rather than being constrained to what he has experienced or what is before him. The child can now think of possible variables and even deduce potential relationships that can later be verified by experiment or observation. Intellectual operations now appear to be predicated upon the same kinds of logical operations that are the stock in trade of the logician, the scientist, or the abstract thinker. It is at this point that the child is able to give formal or axiomatic expression to the concrete ideas that before guided his problem-solving but could not be described or formally understood.

Earlier, while the child is in the stage of concrete operations, he is capable of grasping intuitively and concretely a great many of the basic ideas of mathematics, the sciences, the humanities, and the social sciences. But he can do so only in terms of concrete operations. It can be demonstrated that fifth-grade children can play mathematical games with rules modeled on highly advanced mathematics; indeed, they can arrive at these rules inductively and learn how to work with them. They will flounder, however, if one attempts to force upon them a formal mathematical description of what they have been doing, though they are perfectly capable of guiding their behavior by these rules. At the Woods Hole Conference we were privileged to see a demonstration of teaching in which fifth-grade children very rapidly grasped central ideas from the theory of functions, although had the teacher attempted to explain to them what the theory of functions was, he would have drawn a blank. Later, at the appropriate stage of development and given a certain amount of practice in concrete operations, the time would be ripe for introducing them to the necessary formalism.

What is most important for teaching basic concepts is that the child be helped to pass progressively from concrete thinking to the utilization of more conceptually adequate modes of thought. But it is futile to attempt this by presenting formal explanations based on a logic that is distant from the child's manner of thinking and sterile in its implications for him. Much teaching in mathematics is of this sort. The child learns not to understand mathematical order but rather to apply certain devices or recipes without understanding their significance and connectedness. They are not translated into his way of thinking. Given this inappropriate start, he is easily led to believe that the important thing is for him to be "accurate"—though accuracy has less to do with mathematics than with computation. Perhaps the most striking example of this type of thing is to be found in the manner in which the high school student meets Euclidian geometry for the first time, as a set of axioms and theorems, without having had some experience with simple geometric configurations and the intuitive means whereby one deals with them. If the child were earlier given the concepts and strategies in the form of intuitive geometry at a level that he could easily follow, he might be far better able to grasp deeply the meaning of the theorems and axioms to which he is exposed later.

But the intellectual development of the child is no clockwork sequence of events; it also responds to influences from the environment, notably the school environment. Thus instruction in scientific ideas, even at the elementary level, need not follow slavishly the natural course of cognitive development in the child. It can also lead intellectual development by providing challenging but usable opportunities for the child to forge ahead in his development. Experience has shown that it is worth the effort to provide the growing child with problems that tempt him into next stages of development. As David Page, one of the most experienced teachers of elementary mathematics, has commented: "In teaching from kindergarten to graduate school, I have been amazed at the intellectual similarity of human beings at all ages, although children are perhaps more spontaneous, creative, and energetic than adults. As far as I am concerned young children learn almost anything faster than adults do if it can be given to them in terms they understand. Giving the material to them in terms they understand, interestingly enough, turns out to involve knowing the mathematics oneself, and the better one knows it, the better it can be taught. It is appropriate that we warn ourselves to be careful of assigning an absolute level of difficulty to any particular topic. When I tell mathematicians that fourth-grade students can go a long way into 'set theory' a few of them reply: 'Of course.' Most of them are startled. The latter ones are completely wrong in assuming that 'set theory' is intrinsically difficult. Of course it may be that nothing is intrinsically difficult. We just have to wait until the proper point of view and corresponding language for presenting it are revealed. Given particular subject matter or a particular concept, it is easy to ask trivial questions or to lead the child to ask trivial questions. It is also easy to ask impossibly difficult questions. The trick is to find the medium questions that can be answered and that take you somewhere. This is the big job of teachers and textbooks." One leads the child by the well-wrought "medium questions" to move more rapidly through the stages of intellectual development, to a deeper understanding of mathematical, physical, and historical principles. We must know far more about the ways in which this can be done.

MARTIN BUBER

Martin Buber was born in Vienna, Austria, on February 8, 1878. His early life was spent in Poland with his grandfather, Solomon Buber, an outstanding scholar of Judaism. He studied in Lwow and later at the universities of Vienna, Berlin, Leipzig, and Zurich.

Buber joined the staff of the Zionist periodical *Die Welt* in 1901, but later left the Zionist movement in favor of the Hasidim movement. Beginning in 1904 he withdrew from writing and teaching to study the Hasidic writings. In 1916 he reasserted his interest in Zionism, though his interest was now colored by a profound concern for the community. From 1916 to 1923 he served as editor of *Der Jude*.

In 1923 Buber accepted an appointment to the chair of Jewish philosophy at the University of Frankfurt. In 1938 he went to Israel to teach social philosophy at Hebrew University where he remained until 1951. He died in Jerusalem on June 13, 1965.

Buber has contributed a significant amount of attention to education in such writings as *I and Thou, A Believing Humanism: My Testament, 1902-1905, Between Man and Man,* and *Pointing the Way: Collected Essays.*

Buber feels that education is a personal relationship between the teacher and the student, and believes that modern education more often treats the student as an object to be manipulated by the teacher. Teaching, Buber believes, is an art, not a science, and it should be purposeful art. Primarily, Buber feels that education should not mold students, but should assist them in discovering things about God and the world.

I AND THOU

Martin Buber

AS EXPERIENCE, the world belongs to the primary word *I-It*. The primary word *I-Thou* establishes the world of relation.

*   *   *

If I face a human being as my *Thou*, and say the primary word *I-Thou* to him, he is not a thing among things, and does not consist of things.

Thus human being is not *He* or *She*, bounded from every other *He* and *She*, a specific point in space and time within the net of the world; nor is he a nature able to be experienced and described, a loose bundle of named qualities. But with no neighbor, and whole in himself, he is *Thou* and fills the heavens. This does not mean that nothing exists himself. But all else lives in *his* light.

Just as the melody is not made up of notes nor the verse of words nor the statue of lines, but they must be tugged and dragged till their unity has been scattered into these many pieces, so with the man to whom I say *Thou*. I can take out from him the color of his hair, or of his speech, or of his goodness. I must continually do this. But each time I do it he ceases to be *Thou*.

And just as prayer is not in time but time in prayer, sacrifice not in space but space in sacrifice, and to reverse the relation is to abolish the reality, so with the man to whom I say *Thou*. I do not meet with him at some time and place or other. I can set him in a particular time and place; I must continually do it: but I set only a *He* or a *She*, that is an *It*, no longer my *Thou*.

So long as the heaven of *Thou* is spread out over me the winds of causality cower at my heels, and the whirlpool of fate stays its course.

I do not experience the man to whom I say *Thou*. But I take my stand in relation to him, in the sanctity of the primary word. Only when I step out of it do I experience him once more. In the act of experience *Thou* is far away.

Even if the man to whom I say *Thou* is not aware of it in the midst of his experience, yet relation may exist. For *Thou* is more than *It* realises. No deception penetrates here; here is the cradle of the Real Life.

* * *

The question is, how is it with the *I-Thou* relationship between men? Is it always entirely reciprocal? Can it always be, may it always be? Is it not—like everything human—delivered up to limitation by our insufficiency, and also placed under limitation by the inner laws of our life together?

The first of these two hindrances is well enough known. From your own glance, day by day, into the eyes which look out in estrangement of your "neighbor" who nevertheless does need you, to the melancholy of holy men who time and again vainly offered the great gift—everything tells you that full mutuality is not inherent in men's life together. It is a grace, for which one must always be ready and which one never gains as an assured possession.

Yet there are some *I-Thou* relationships which in their nature may not unfold to full mutuality if they are to persist in that nature.

Elsewhere[1] I have characterized the relationship of the genuine educator to his pupil as being a relationship of this kind. In order to help the realization of the best potentialities in the pupil's life, the teacher must really *mean* him as the definite person he is in his potentiality and his actuality; more precisely, he must not know him as a mere sum of qualities, strivings and inhibitions, he must be aware of him as a whole being and affirm him in this wholeness. But he can only do this if he meets him again and again as his partner in a bipolar situation. And in order that his effect upon him may be a unified and significant one he

---

[1] "Education," section III of *Between Man and Man*.

must also live this situation, again and again, in all its moments not merely from his own end but also from that of his partner: he must practise the kind of realization which I call inclusion (*Umfassung*).

But however much depends upon his awakening the *I-Thou* relationship in the pupil as well—and however much depends upon the pupil, too, meaning and affirming him as the particular person he is—the special educative relation could not persist if the pupil for his part practised "inclusion," that is, if he lived the teacher's part in the common situation. Whether the *I-Thou* relationship now comes to an end or assumes the quite different character of a friendship, it is plain that the specifically educative as such is denied full mutuality.

Another no less illuminating example of the normative limitation of mutuality is presented to us in the relation between a genuine psychotherapist and his patient. If he is satisfied to "analyse" him, i.e. to bring to light unknown factors from his microcosm and to set to some conscious work in life the energies which have been transformed by such an emergence then he may be successful in some repair work. At best he may help a soul which is diffused and poor in structure to collect and order itself to some extent. But the real matter, the regeneration of an atrophied personal center, will not be achieved. This can only be done by one who grasps the buried latent unity of the suffering soul with the great glance of the doctor: and this can only be attained in the person-to-person attitude of a partner, not by the consideration and examination of an object. In order that he may coherently further the liberation and actualization of that unity in a new accord of the person with the world, the psychotherapist, like the educator, must stand again and again not merely at his own pole in the bipolar relation, but also with the strength of present realization at the other pole, and experience the effect of his own action. But again, the specific "healing" relation would come to an end the moment the patient thought of, and succeeded in, practising "inclusion" and experiencing the event from the doctor's pole as well. Healing, like educating, is only possible to the one who lives over against the other, and yet is detached.[2]

The most emphatic example of normative limitation of mutuality could be provided by the pastor with a cure of souls, for in this instance an

---

[2] Cf. Martin Buber, *Pointing the Way: Collected Essays*, ed. and tr. by Maurice Friedman (New York: Harpers, 1957), "Healing Through Meeting," pp. 93-97. See also Martin Buber, "Guilt and Guilt Feelings," tr. by M. Friedman, *Psychiatry, ibid.*

"inclusion" coming from the other side would attack the sacral authenticity of the commission.

Every *I-Thou* relationship, within a relation which is specified as a purposive working of one part upon the other, persists in virtue of a mutuality which is forbidden to be full.

In this context only one question more must be discussed, but it must be discussed since it is incomparably the most important of all.

The question is, how can the eternal *Thou* in the relation be at once exclusive and inclusive? How can the *Thou*-relationship of man to God, which is conditioned by an unconditioned turning to him, diverted by nothing, nevertheless include all other *I-Thou* relations of this man, and bring them as it were to God?

Note that the question is not about God, but about our relation to him. And yet in order to be able to answer I must speak of him. For our relation to him is as above contradictions as it is, because he is as above contradictions as he is.

Of course we speak only of what God is in his relation to a man. And even that is only to be expressed in paradox; more precisely, by the paradoxical use of a concept; more precisely still, by the paradoxical combination of a substantive concept with an adjective which contradicts its normal content. The assertion of this contradiction must yield to the insight that the indispensable description of the object by this concept can be justified only in this way. The content of the concept is revolutionized, transformed, and extended—but this is indeed what we experience with every concept which we take out of immanence—compelled by the reality of faith—and use with reference to the working of transcendence.

The description of God as a Person is indispensable for everyone who like myself means by "God" not a principle (although mystics like Eckhart sometimes identify him with "Being") and like myself means by "God" not an idea (although philosophers like Plato at times could hold that he was this): but who rather means by "God," as I do, him who—whatever else he may be—enters into a direct relation with us men in creative, revealing and redeeming acts, and thus makes it possible for us to enter into a direct relation with him. This ground and meaning of our existence constitutes a mutuality, arising again and again, such as can subsist only between persons. The concept of personal being is indeed completely incapable of declaring what God's essential being is, but it is both permitted and necessary to say that God is *also* a Person. If as an exception I wished to translate what is meant by this into philosophical language, that of Spinoza, I should have to say that of God's infinitely many attributes we men do not know two, as Spinoza thinks, but three: to spiritual being (in which is to be found the source of what we call spirit) and to natural being (which presents itself in what is known to us as nature) would be added the attribute of personal being. From this attribute would stem my and all men's being as person, as from those other attributes would stem my and all men's being as spirit and being as nature. And only this third attribute of personal being would be given to us to be known direct in its quality as an attribute.

But now the contradiction appears in the appeal to the familiar content of the concept person. This says that it is indeed the property of a person that its independence should consist in itself, but that it is limited in its total being by the plurality of other independent entities; and this can of course not be true of God. This contradiction is countered by the paradoxical description of God as the absolute Person, i.e., the Person who cannot be limited. It is as the absolute Person that God enters into direct relation with us. The contradiction yields to deeper insight.

As a Person God gives personal life, he makes us as persons become capable of meeting with him and with one another. But no limitation can come upon him as the absolute Person, either from us or from our relations with one another; in fact we can dedicate to him not merely our persons but also our relations to one another. The man who turns to him therefore need not turn away from any other *I-Thou* relation; but he properly brings them to him, and lets them be fulfilled "in the face of God."

One must, however, take care not to understand this conversation with God—the conversation of which I have to speak in this book and in almost all the works which followed—as something happening solely alongside or above the everyday. God's speech to men penetrates what happens in the life of each one of us, and all that happens in the world around us, biographical and historical, and makes it for you and me into instruction, message, demand. Happening upon happening, situation upon situation, are enabled and empowered by the personal speech of God to demand of the human person that he take his stand and make his decision. Often enough we think there is nothing to hear, but long before we have ourselves put wax in our ears.

The existence of mutuality between God and man cannot be proved, just as God's existence cannot be proved. Yet he who dares to speak of it, bears witness, and calls to witness him to whom he speaks—whether that witness is now or in the future.

JAMES BRYANT CONANT

James Bryant Conant was born on March 24, 1893, in Dorchester, Massachusetts. He went to public kindergarten, then after a brief experience in a private school entered the third grade in the Bailey Street Public School. After graduation from high school he entered Harvard University in 1910. He completed his undergraduate studies in three years, was elected to Phi Beta Kappa, and became an honorary John Harvard Scholar. Without stopping for a master's examination he received a Ph.D. in chemistry in 1916. He began to teach at Harvard in 1914, and after taking time out for a brief stint in Washington with the Chemical Warfare Service he returned to teaching chemistry at Harvard. In 1933 he was named to the presidency of Harvard University, and he held this position until 1953.

From 1955 to 1957 Conant served as United States Ambassador to the Federal Republic of West Germany, and after leaving that post began an extensive study of American education. Some of his books about education include The American High School Today, Education and Liberty, Shaping Educational Policy, and The Education of American Teachers.

Conant has made a number of suggestions for the renovation of American education. He has given a great deal of attention, not only to the problems of curriculum and instruction in American education, but to the problems of building and financing as well. Conant has made a number of proposals for education, and many of them have already been accepted into practice. His continuing efforts to reform American education have won him a devoted number of followers.

THE CITADEL OF LEARNING

James Bryant Conant

If I am right in my interpretation of the past, the fluidity of American society and the democratic ideals of the nation were primarily responsible for shaping educational policy in the United States. I believe that a careful student of this country 125 years ago could have come very close to predicting what our present schools and colleges would be like. Indeed, it seems to me, much of what de Tocqueville admired and much of what he questioned in the United States of his day, when translated into terms of schools and universities, is what we find typically American at this moment. The burgeoning pioneer republic, assimilating a variety of national cultures, and combining the industrial revolution with an expanding agriculture, was bound to produce some strange cultural institutions—that is to say, strange as seen through European eyes. But these institutions were not only a product of the new forces by themselves powerful factors in directing the course of our internal history. The men and women trained in the new types of schools, colleges, and universities in the first three decades of this century are the men and women who largely determine the present cultural pattern of the United States.

Some of us can well remember how in the early 1930's our academic friends in England and on the Continent ridiculed the American ideals of equality of opportunity and equality of respect and our belief in the importance of free competition. Outdated pioneer notions, we were told, not germane to the highly industrialized and class-conscious society of the twentieth century. The road to the future, we were assured

James Bryant Conant. *The Citadel of Learning*, Yale University Press, New Haven, Conn., 1956, pp. 33-47. © 1956 by Yale University Press and reprinted by permission.

by the European radicals of that day, was a socialistic one. It has turned out quite otherwise. Here in America in the last twenty-five years we have evolved a type of economic and social system that was predicted by few European observers. Paul Hoffman has called it "mutual capitalism." Clarence Randall has written about it as follows:

"The United States is a miracle among nations . . . we are still sound financially and all about us we see abundant evidence of constantly rising standards of living. We surge ahead with a vitality and confidence in the future that amaze the world. We do this because we release the unbounded potential for effort of each individual citizen, by rewarding him in accordance with his effort, and by stimulating his imagination through the widest possible freedom of choices in his life... We accumulate our resources by rewarding those who produce and save; we restrain selfishness by competition.

"It is no coincidence," he continues, "that our economic way of life and our high standard of living are found together." To which I venture to add that it is no coincidence that our economic way of life and our unique American tradition of education are found together. The internal development of this nation politically, socially, and economically has been bound up with the unfolding of a characteristic American point of view about schools, colleges, and universities.

A century ago American education started to adapt itself to a set of new conditions and succeeded. Today, we face a totally different task. Within a decade this nation has been thrust into a position of enormous responsibility in a highly uncomfortable new world. A century ago the ideas of schools and universities imported from Europe had to be drastically modified to suit the needs of a new type of nation based on new geographic facts and motivated by new ideals. Does the American tradition in education, now approaching the respectable age of one hundred years, likewise stand in need of modification to meet the challenge of our new world, the constricted globe of the mid-twentieth century? My answer would be an emphatic yes. For it seems clear to me that the world conditions we Americans face today are as different from those of ten or twenty years ago as were the conditions faced by our grandparents compared with those of Europe. The contrast now is not between a new nation in process of expanding and older static nations. The contrast now is between the isolated United States of a relatively few years ago, able to struggle through its own social, political, and economic problems largely independent of Europe or of Asia, and a United States one of the two great powers in a world where long distances have disappeared.

Those who remember the "Gay Twenties" would probably agree that the contrast between the third and the sixth decades of this century is for Americans a contrast not of degree but of kind. Whether we like it or not (and there are few in my age group who fail to dislike it at least some of the time) we are living cheek by jowl with some new neighbors, some friendly and helpful, others not. Thanks to the modern airplane, we find ourselves now in much the same situation that Europeans have known for centuries.

It would have been difficult enough for us Americans to accustom ourselves to a globe on which the Atlantic and Pacific Oceans were the equivalent of narrow channels, and the polar regions no longer unexplored and inaccessible. But we must adjust ourselves to a new geography in a period characterized by two phrases, the one hardly less ominous than the other—"a divided world" and "an era of nuclear weapons."

I have no intention of exploring here the implications for the United States that lie hidden in the words "a divided world," but I do want to stress the significance for American education of the altered geography of this age. If, by some miracle, nuclear weapons could be brought under international control and thus eliminated from our thoughts, man's ability to travel through the air at the rate of hundreds of miles an hour would remain unchanged. If the Soviet power should crumble and the Communist bloc disintegrate tomorrow, the American people would still be living under conditions so different from those of a few decades ago as to warrant the use of the phrase "new world." It is, first of all, these conditions that must call forth an imaginative response on the part of our teachers and educational leaders. That this will come, I feel confident. Just as the new conditions in the mid-nineteenth century resulted in the founding of agricultural and mechanical arts colleges and the passage of the land-grant act (Morrill Act) of 1862, so, too, the new conditions of the twentieth century will bring about another American educational transformation.

As long as the world remains divided, we have a very special and heavy responsibility. We are the acknowledged leader of the free nations. Because of our size and our wealth we are the prime defender of all that is involved in the opposition of these free nations to the Soviet ideology. Our schools, colleges, and universities are conscious of the implication for education of this responsibility. The nature of the opposition between the doctrines we hold dear and those of the totalitarian Communist regime must be made clear; this is being done as part of the work of educating our future citizens for life in the American democracy. This job, I have reason to believe, is already well in hand. I have no doubt this phase of American education will continue. But I am not so sure that in certain other respects American education has started even to outline the problems which the new geography has forced upon it.

We have acquired for the first time many near neighbors. A hard-headed appraisal of these neighbors is obviously of first importance. To lay the groundwork for such an appraisal is one of the new tasks of American education. I am well aware of the fact that for many years some educators have urged that our schools and colleges be more concerned with international affairs. But to be quite frank, much of what was written on this subject before the end of World War II is worse than obsolete. The hard realities of the situation in which we now live were not foreseen by those who were active in these affairs ten years ago.

First, let us consider the impact of the new tasks on general education. Our future citizens must know what it means to know thoroughly a friendly or a hostile neighbor. We must develop a higher degree of sophistication about foreign affairs, avoiding optimistic sentimentality on the one hand and hopeless cynicism on the other. We need large numbers of men and women who, without themselves being prepared to appraise a foreign nation, realize some of the complexities and difficulties of the task. In this field as in so many others today, it is easy to form a superficial judgment, difficult to grasp what are the essential facts that the experts themselves must come to grip with.

Just as we need an understanding of the way science has developed in order to evaluate the statements of scientific experts, so I think the proverbial man in the street needs an understanding of the way national interests in the past have developed and interlocked. Specificially, this means a far greater emphasis on the study of history. I have long advocated that special attention should be paid in schools and colleges to American history. In the past, I have thought of this largely as internal political and social history. It now seems clear that foreign policy requires at least as much study. And a consideration of the foreign policy of the United States, of course, takes one automatically into the foreign policy of other nations.

More important than the changes in general education will be, I am sure, the changes in specialized education. One obvious example: We need for the first time in our history a very large number of highly competent men and women with talents and tastes for work with people of foreign lands. We shall need to discover such people at an earlier age and provide the educational opportunities for their development. This in part is a question of acquiring skills—the command of foreign tongues —but also of the development of an interest in other lands and peoples. All of which means a vast amount of hard work, long hours of study, patient labor with the printed as well as the spoken word.

In this connection, another look at Europe may not be out of order. Geography to no small degree has moulded the European concept of what is required of the schools in the way of teaching skills. Holland and Switzerland illustrate the point I have in mind. In those countries no one is considered educated who cannot speak fluently at least two foreign languages (and I emphasize the phrase at least). The revolution in transportation has made the capitals of France, Germany, Italy, and Spain almost as close to Washington as those capitals were to each other at the time of World War I. I need labor the point no further. That the place of foreign language instruction, like the place of history, in the future curricula of American schools will be very different from the past is an obvious prediction. That this change will make schooldays easier not even the most enthusiastic linguist is likely to maintain. The new position of the United States of a shrunken globe places new burdens on all of us, including all our youths.

The demands of military service in themselves are having, and will continue to have, a great effect on our educational institutions. But quite apart from these considerations which apply to our able-bodied young men, the burden is on all our young people, men and women alike. Their potential capacities are this nation's greatest asset. The time of youth is the time for developing these capacities; to the extent this time is wasted, America of the future will be poorer, less able to shoulder the heavy loads the new world conditions place upon us. And even the most enthusiastic supporter of American education must admit that a great deal of time is wasted in school and college.

In 1950 the Educational Policies Commission of the National Education Association published a pamphlet entitled EDUCATION OF THE GIFTED. In the foreword it was stated, "Acquaintance with present educational practices has convinced the Commission that the gifted members of the total school population constitute a minority which is too largely neglected." It would be out of place for me to detail the recommendations of this report, though I am tempted to do so, as I was one of its authors. But I can sum up what we had in mind by quoting the following sentence: "To capitalize the rich resources of human talent which gifted children and youth possess, the schools and colleges must give special attention to the education of their gifted students."

This call to the schools and colleges was written before it was as clear as now what the nature of the postwar period would be. The last five years have spelled out for us the consequences of living in a constricted yet divided world. These consequences surely underline the need for educational reforms in regard to gifted children. For in this difficult period, if the United States is to fulfill its role, it will need to utilize to the fullest possible extent "the rich resources of human talent" in each generation.

Let me give two examples: There has been an increasing concern in recent years with our failure to educate a sufficient number of scientists and engineers. That is to say, a number sufficient to man adequately our industries and our national defense establishments. The colleges blame the schools for inadequate preparation (particularly in mathematics), and the schools blame the taxpayers for not providing sufficient funds to pay for first-rate teachers of science and mathematics. Both criticisms are correct to my way of thinking; as to the second, I shall have more to say in the concluding pages of this book. As to the first, the difficulty is in no small part due to our failure to identify at a relatively young age those boys and girls who have more than the average talent for mathematics. If such pupils were identified (and tests for this purpose seem to be at hand) and then were stimulated to proceed relatively rapidly with their studies, a respectable fraction of the incoming freshmen of the better colleges would have sufficient mathematical aptitude to tackle the physics and chemistry courses with both enthusiasm and success. At present, a number of college students who formerly had the ambition of becoming scientists drop out once they run into the difficulties of freshman physics, chemistry, and mathematics.

Similar considerations apply to the study of foreign languages. As in the case of mathematics I doubt the wisdom of attempting to force any large proportion of our high school students into the type of "stiff" courses of instruction characteristic of the European university preparatory schools. It is true that lack of native ability may to a considerable degree be compensated for by diligent study. But the social pressures which in Europe have forced the students headed for a university to work extremely hard at school (by American standards) do not exist in the United States and are not likely to exist in the near future. Too many American families (even in the higher income brackets) ask the headmaster (even of a private school), Why should Johnny have to continue with mathematics, which is so hard for him? After all, we don't want him to be an Einstein! And as for foreign languages, why should our son keep on with his French, when, as far as anyone can tell, he may never need it? The parental demand for a "thorough" European type of education hardly exists in the United States even among the 5 or 10 per cent of the population whose sons in older countries would be forced "willy-nilly" to study what they were told to and not necessarily what they like. And in the American public school as well as in the private college-preparatory school, the attitude of the student is not conducive to taking on hard tasks of "book learning" because someone in authority says it is important. American sons and daughters, unlike their European counterparts, have learned at a young age to ask and demand a rational answer to the question "Why should I do that?"

The way out of this educational quandary lies in identifying scholastic talent young (in mathematics or foreign languages or both) and then providing for teachers who will stimulate the selected students to do their utmost because they want to and as a matter of pride. The colleges must do their part by accepting the selected students on such a basis that their unusual high school accomplishments will be recognized and suitably rewarded. The spirit of competition is not, to my mind, something to be deplored. If kept in bounds by a spirit of "fair play," it is a healthy aspect of our tremendous emphasis on sports. There is no reason why the same type of motivation could not be utilized in the study of mathematics and foreign languages, provided, as in athletics, selection of the naturally talented is accepted as a matter of course; and provided that public opinion becomes convinced of the importance of the undertaking.

No one expects a majority of school children to learn to play a musical instrument, but nearly everyone would like to have the musically gifted encouraged to develop their talents. Our attitude toward music might well serve as a pattern as to the attitude which we Americans should take in regard to the education of our youth whose native ability lies in the fields of words or numbers. Local enthusiasm needs to be aroused for discovering and adequately educating those who are intellectually gifted. On a national scale the recently established Merit Scholarship Corporation is an important step in this direction. Identification of talent, motivation through aroused interest and competition should enable our schools to utilize much more than now the rich sources of talent in each generation.

What I have just suggested and the changes I shall later propose for our colleges and universities can be accomplished by modifications in our educational practices so slight that they will not jeopardize the essence of the American tradition in education. We need not retreat one step from our own goal of providing education for all (and I mean all) American youth. For, let me make it plain, I am neither prophesying nor recommending abandonment of those basic principles that characterize our schools and colleges as contrasted with the European. Equality of opportunity for all children and equality of respect among all occupational groups are two doctrines that are as significant for our future as for our past. These are the fundamental promises of American education. Every citizen needs to understand them; every citizen needs to realize how they differ from the promises in other lands. He will then be more ready to support in every possible way the further development of the American tradition of education and to adapt it to the new world. If one understands why American schools have developed as they have, one will be the more ready to support those schools in such a way as to make them correspond to the needs of the new world in which we live.

PAUL GOODMAN

Paul Goodman was born on September 9, 1911, in New York City, where he says that he was reared in the jungles of New York and the wilds of the Hudson River. He attended elementary and secondary schools in New York City, and in 1927 he graduated from Townsend Harris High School at the top of his class. He received his B.A. from City College in 1931, and though he earned a Ph.D. at the University of Chicago in 1940, it was not actually awarded until 1954. He has taught at the University of Chicago, New York University, Black Mountain College, Sarah Lawrence College, and the University of Wisconsin. He has also lectured at many schools throughout the country, and is associated with the New York and Cleveland Institutes for Gestalt Therapy and the University Seminar on Problems of Interpretation at Columbia. He is also a Fellow of the Institute for Policy Studies in Washington, D.C.

Goodman has written for a wide number of magazines including *Politics*, *Partisan Review*, *Liberation*, *Kenyon Review*, *Commentary*, and *Resistance*. His books on education include *Communitas*, written with Percival Goodman, *Compulsory Mis-education*, *The Community of Scholars*, *Growing Up Absurd*, *Five Years*, and *Utopian Essays and Practical Proposals*.

Goodman's chief interest is to find ways to improve and make our environment livable by restoring human scale in modern technological and urban conditions. He has also devoted himself to problems of growth and education, and has worked particularly on the problems of career-block.

Goodman likes much that he finds in Progressive education, but feels that Progressivism, despite its arguments to the contrary, never encouraged students toward solving the major problems of our society. He is tired of education that incarcerates, molds, propagandizes, and turns people into pawns for the establishment. Goodman, who is a self-professed anarchist, is strongly opposed to compulsory education and advocates radical changes in our present methods of education from kindergarten through college.

COMPULSORY MIS-EDUCATION

Paul Goodman

i

A conference of experts on school drop-outs will discuss the background of poverty, cultural deprivation, race prejudice, family and emotional troubles, neighborhood uprooting, urban mobility. It will explore ingenious expedients to counteract these conditions, though it will not much look to remedying them—that is not its business. And it will suggest propaganda—e.g., no school, no job—to get the youngsters back in school. It is axiomatic that they ought to be in school.

After a year, it proves necessary to call another conference to cope with the alarming fact that more than 75% of the drop-outs who have been cajoled into returning, have dropped out again. They persist in failing; they still are not sufficiently motivated. What curricular changes must there be? How can the teachers learn the life-style of the underprivileged?

Curiously muffled in these conferences is the question that puts the burden of proof the other way: What are they drop-outs from? Is the schooling really good for them, or much good for anybody? Since, for many, there are such difficulties with the present arrangements, might not some better arrangements be invented? Or bluntly, since schooling undertakes to be compulsory, must it not continually review its claim to be useful? Is it the only means of education? Isn't it unlikely that *any* single type of social institution could fit almost every youngster up

---

Paul Goodman. *Compulsory Mis-education*, Horizon Press, New York, 1964, pp. 19-42. © 1964 by Paul Goodman and reprinted by permission.

to age 16 and beyond? (It is predicted that by 1970, 50% will go to college.)

But conferences on drop-outs are summoned by school professionals, so perhaps we cannot hope that such elementary questions will be raised. Yet neither are they raised by laymen. There is a mass superstition, underwritten by additional billions every year, that adolescents must continue going to school. The middle class *know* that no professional competence—i.e., status and salary—can be attained without many diplomas; and poor people have allowed themselves to be convinced that the primary remedy for their increasing deprivation is to agitate for better schooling. Nevertheless, I doubt that, *at present or with any reforms that are conceivable under present school administration,* going to school is the best use for the time of life of the majority of youth.

ii

Education is a natural community function and occurs inevitably, since the young grow up on the old, toward their activities, and into (or against) their institutions; and the old foster, teach, train, exploit, and abuse the young. Even neglect of the young, except physical neglect, has an educational effect—not the worst possible.

Formal schooling is a reasonable auxiliary of the inevitable process, whenever an activity is best learned by singling it out or special attention with a special person to teach it. Yet it by no means follows that the complicated artifact of a school system has much to do with education, and certainly not with good education.

Let us bear in mind the way in which a big school system might have nothing to do with education at all. The New York system turns over $700 millions annually, not including capital improvements. There are 750 schools, with perhaps 15 annually being replaced at an extra cost of $2 to $5 millions each. There are 40,000 paid employees. This is a vast vested interest, and it is very probable that—like much of our economy and almost all of our political structure, of which the public schools are a part—it goes on for its own sake, keeping more than a million people busy, wasting wealth, and pre-empting time and space in which something else could be going on. It is a gigantic market for textbook manufacturers, building contractors, and graduate-schools of Education.

The fundamental design of such a system is ancient, yet it has not been altered although the present operation is altogether different in scale from what it was, and therefore it must have a different meaning. For example, in 1900, 6% of the 17-year-olds graduated from high school, and less than ½% went to college; whereas in 1963, 65% graduated from high school and 35% went on to something called college. Likewise, there is a vast difference between schooling intermitted in life on a farm or in a city with plenty of small jobs, and schooling that is a child's only "serious" occupation and often his only adult contact. Thus, a perhaps outmoded institution has become almost the only allowable way of growing up. And with this pre-empting, there is an increasing intensification of the one narrow experience, e.g., in the shaping of the curriculum and testing according to the increasing requirements of graduate schools far off in time and place. Just as our American society as a whole is more and more tightly organized, so its school system is more and more regimented as part of that organization.

In the organizational plan, the schools play a non-educational and an educational role. The non-educational role is very important. In the tender grades, the schools are a baby-sitting service during a period of collapse of the old-type family and during a time of extreme urbanization and urban mobility. In the junior and senior high school grades, they are an arm of the police, providing cops and concentration camps paid for in the budget under the heading "Board of Education." The educational role is, by and large, to provide—at public and parents' expense—apprentice-training for corporations, government, and the teaching professions itself, and also to train the young, as New York's Commissioner of Education has said (in the Worley case), "to handle constructively their problems of adjustment to authority."

The public schools of America have indeed been a powerful, and beneficent, force for the democratizing of a great mixed population. But we must be careful to keep reassessing them when, with changing conditions, they become a universal trap and democracy begins to look like regimentation.

iii

Let me spend a page on the history of the compulsory nature of the school systems. In 1961, in *The Child, the Parent, and the State*, James Conant mentions a possible incompatibility between "individual development" and "national needs"; this, to my mind, is a watershed in

American philosophy of education and puts us back to the ideology of Imperial Germany, or on a par with contemporary Russia.

When Jefferson and Madison conceived of compulsory schooling, such an incompatibility would have been unthinkable. They were in the climate of the Enlightenment, were strongly influenced by Congregational (town-meeting) ideas, and were of course makers of a revolution. To them, "citizen" meant society-*maker*, not one "participating in" or "adjusted to" society. It is clear that they regarded themselves and their friends as citizens existentially, so to speak; to make society was their breath of life. But obviously such conceptions are worlds removed from, and diametrically opposed to, our present political reality, where the ground rules and often the score are pre-determined.

For Jefferson, people had to be taught in order to multiply the sources of citizenly initiative and to be vigilant for freedom. Everybody had to become literate and study history, in order to make constitutional innovations and be fired to defend free institutions, which was presumably the moral that history taught. And those of good parts were to study a technological natural philosophy, in order to make inventions and produce useful goods for the new country. By contrast, what are the citizenly reasons for which we compel everybody to be literate, etc.? To keep the economy expanding, to understand the mass-communications, to choose between indistinguishable Democrats and Republicans. Planning and decision-making are lodged in top managers; rarely, and at most, the electorate serves as a pressure-group. There is a new emphasis on teaching science—we will discuss this in another context—but the vast majority will never use this knowledge and will forget it; they are consumers.

Another great impulse for compulsory education came from the new industrialism and urbanism during the three or four decades after the Civil War, a time also of maximum immigration. Here the curricular demands were more mundane: in the grades, literacy and arithmetic; in the colleges, professional skills to man the expanding economy. But again, no one would have spoken of an incompatibility between "individual development" and "national needs," for it was considered to be an open society, abounding in opportunity. Typically, the novels of Horatio Alger, Jr., treat schooling as morally excellent as well as essential for getting ahead; and there is no doubt that the immigrants saw education-for-success as also a human value for their children. Further, the school-system was not a trap. The 94% who in 1900 did not finish high school had other life opportunities, including making a lot of money and rising in politics. But again, by and large this is not our present situation. There is plenty of social mobility, opportunity to rise—except precisely for the ethnic minorities who are our main concern as drop-outs—but the statuses and channels are increasingly stratified, rigidified, cut and dried. Most enterprise is parceled out by feudal corporations, or by the state; and these determine the requirements. Ambition with average talent meets these rules or fails; those without relevant talent, or with unfortunate backgrounds, cannot even survive in decent poverty. The requirements of survival are importantly academic, attainable only in schools and universities; but such schooling is ceasing to have an initiating or moral meaning.

We do not have an open economy; even when jobs are not scarce, the corporations and state dictate the possibilities of enterprise. General Electric swoops down on the high schools, or IBM on the colleges, and skims off the youth who have been pre-trained for them at public or private expense. (Private college tuition runs upward of $6000, and this is estimated as a third or less of the actual cost for "education and educational administration." Even a department store requires a diploma for its salespeople, not so much because of the skills they have learned as that it guarantees the right character: punctual and with a smooth record. And more generally, since our powers-that-be have opted for an expanding economy with a galloping standard of living, and since the powers of the world are in an arms and space race, there *is* a national need for many graduates specifically trained. Thus, even for those selected, the purpose is irrelevant to citizenly initiative, the progress of an open society, or personal happiness, and the others have spent time and effort in order to be progressively weeded out. Some drop out.

iv

It is said that our schools are geared to "middle-class values," but this is a false and misleading use of terms. The schools less and less represent *any* human values, but simply adjustment to a mechanical system.

Because of the increasing failure of the schools with the poor urban mass, there has developed a line of criticism—e.g., Oscar Lewis, Patricia Sexton, Frank Riessman, and even Edgar Friedenberg—asserting that there is a "culture of poverty" which the "middle-class" schools do not fit, but which has its own virtues of spontaneity, sociality, animality. The implication is that the "middle-class," for all its virtues, is obsessional, prejudiced, prudish.

Pedagogically, this insight is indispensable. A teacher must try to reach each child in terms of what he brings, his background, his habits, the language he understands. But if taken to be more than technical, it is a disastrous conception. The philosophic aim of education must be to get each one out of his isolated class and into the one humanity. Prudence and responsibility are not middle-class virtues but human virtues; and spontaneity and sexuality are not powers of the simple but of human health. One has the impression that our social-psychologists are looking not to a human community but to a future in which the obsessionals will take care of the impulsives!

In fact, some of the most important strengths that have historically belonged to the middle class are flouted by the schools: independence, initiative, scrupulous honesty, earnestness, utility, respect for thorough scholarship. Rather than bourgeois, our schools have become petty-bourgeois, bureaucratic, time-serving, gradgrind-practical, timid, and *nouveau riche* climbing. In the upper grades and colleges, they often exude a cynicism that belongs to rotten aristocrats.

Naturally, however, the youth of the poor and of the middle-class respond differently to the petty bourgeois atmosphere. For many poor children, school is orderly and has food, compared to chaotic and hungry homes, and it might even be interesting compared to total deprivation of toys and books. Besides, the wish to improve a child's lot, which on the part of a middle-class parent might be frantic status-seeking and pressuring, on the part of a poor parent is a loving aspiration. There is here a gloomy irony. The school that for a poor Negro child might be a great joy and opportunity is likely to be dreadful; whereas the middle-class child might be better off *not* in the "good" surburban school he has.

Other poor youth, herded into a situation that does not fit their disposition, for which they are unprepared by their background, and which does not interest them, simply develop a reactive stupidity very different from their behavior on the street or ball field. They fall behind, play truant, and as soon as possible drop out. If the school situation is immediately useless and damaging to them, their response must be said to be life-preservative. They thereby somewhat diminish their chances of a decent living, but we shall see that the usual propaganda —that schooling is a road to high salaries—is for most poor youth a lie; and the increase in security is arguably not worth the torture involved.

The reasonable social policy would be not to have these youth in school, certainly not in high school, but to educate them otherwise and provide opportunity for a decent future in some other way. How? I shall venture some suggestions later; in my opinion, the wise thing would be to have our conferences on *this* issue, and omit the idea of drop-out altogether. But the brute fact is that our society isn't really interested; the concern for the drop-outs is mainly because they are a nuisance and a threat and can't be socialized by the existing machinery.

Numerically far more important than these overt drop-outs at 16, however, are the children who conform to schooling between the ages of 6 to 16 or 20, but who drop out internally and day-dream, their days wasted, their liberty caged and scheduled. And there are many such in the middle class, from backgrounds with plenty of food and some books and art, where the youth is seduced by the prospect of money and status, but even more where he is terrified to jeopardize the only pattern of life he knows.

It is in the schools and from the mass media, rather than at home or from their friends, that the mass of our citizens in all classes learn that life is inevitably routine, depersonalized, venally graded; that it is best to toe the mark and shut up; that there is no place for spontaneity, open sexuality, free spirit. Trained in the schools, they go on to the same quality of jobs, culture, politics. This IS education, mis-education, socializing to the national norms and regimenting to the national "needs."

John Dewey used to hope, naïvely, that the schools could be a community somewhat better than society and serve as a lever for social change. In fact, our schools reflect our society closely, except that they *emphasize* many of its worst features, as well as having the characteristic defects of academic institutions of all times and places.

v

Let us examine realistically half a dozen aspects of the school that is dropped out *from.*

(a) There is widespread anxiety about the children not learning to read, and hot and defensive argument about the methods of teaching

69

reading. Indeed, reading deficiency is an accumulating scholastic disadvantage that results in painful feelings of inferiority, truancy, and drop-out. Reading is crucial for school success—all subjects depend on it—and therefore for the status-success that the diploma is about. Yet in all anxiety and argument, there is no longer any mention of the freedom and human cultivation that literacy is supposed to stand for.

In my opinion, there is something phony here. For a change, let us look at this "reading" coldly and ask if it is really such a big deal except precisely in the school that is supposed to teach it and is sometimes failing to do so.

With the movies, TV, and radio that the illiterate also share, there is certainly no lack of "communications." We cannot say that as humanities of science, the reading-matter of the great majority is in any way superior to the content of these other media. And in the present stage of technology and economy, it is probably *less* true than it was in the late nineteenth century—the time of the great push to universal literacy and arithmetic—that the mass-teaching of reading is indispensable to operate the production and clerical system. It is rather our kind of urbanism, politics, and buying and selling that require literacy. These are not excellent.

Perhaps in the present dispensation we should be as well off if it were socially acceptable for large numbers not to read. It would be harder to regiment people if they were not so well "informed"; as Norbert Wiener used to point out, every repetition of a cliché only increases the noise and *prevents* communication. With less literacy, there would be more folk culture. Much suffering of inferiority would be avoided if youngsters did not have to meet a perhaps unnecessary standard. Serious letters could only benefit if society were less swamped by trash, lies, and bland verbiage. Most important of all, *more* people might become genuinely literate if it were understood that reading is not a matter-of-course but a *special useful art with a proper subject-matter, imagination and truth*, rather than a means of communicating top-down decisions and advertising. (The advertising is a typical instance: when the purpose of advertising was to give information—"New shipment of salt fish arrived, very good, foot of Barclay Street"—it was useful to be able to read; when the point of advertising is to create a synthetic demand, it is better not to be able to read.)

(b) Given their present motives, the schools are not competent to teach authentic literacy, reading as a means of liberation and cultivation. And I doubt that most of us who seriously read and write the English language ever learned it by the route of "Run, Spot, Run" to *Silas Marner*. Rather, having picked up the rudiments either in cultured homes or in the first two grades, we really learned to read by our own will and free exploration, following our bent, generally among books that are considered inappropriate by school librarians!

A great neurologist tells me that the puzzle is not how to teach reading, but why some children fail to learn to read. Given the amount of exposure that any urban child gets, any normal animal should spontaneously catch on to the code. What prevents? It is almost demonstrable that, for many children, it is precisely going to school that prevents —because of the school's alien style, banning of spontaneous interest, extrinsic rewards and punishments. (In many underprivileged schools, the I.Q. steadily falls the longer they go to school.) Many of the backward readers might have had a better chance on the streets.

But let me say something, too, about the "successful" teaching of reading and writing in the schools. Consider, by contrast, the method employed by Sylvia Ashton-Warner in teaching little Maoris. She gets them to ask for their *own* words, the particular gut-word of fear, lust, or despair that is obsessing the child that day; this is written for him on strong cardboard; he learns it instantaneously and never forgets it; and soon he has an exciting, if odd, vocabulary. From the beginning, writing is by demand, practical, magical; and of course it is simply an extension of speech—it is the best and strongest speech, as writing should be. What is read is what somebody is importantly trying to tell. Now what do our schools do? We use tricks of mechanical conditioning. These do positive damage to spontaneous speech, meant expression, earnest understanding. Inevitably, they create *in the majority* the wooden attitude toward "writing," as entirely different from speech, that college-teachers later try to cope with in Freshman Composition. And reading inevitably becomes a manipulation of signs, e.g., for test-passing, that has no relation to experience.

(Until recently, the same discouragement by school-teachers plagued children's musical and plastic expression, but there have been attempts to get back to spontaneity—largely, I think, because of the general revolution in modern art and musical theory. In teaching science, there is just now a strong movement to encourage imagination rather than conditioned "answers." In teaching foreign languages, the emphasis is now strongly on vital engagement and need to speak. Yet in teaching reading and writing, the direction has been the contrary; even progressive education has gone back to teaching spelling. These arts are regarded merely as "tools.")

(c) The young rightly resist animal constraint. But, at least in New York where I have been a school-board Visitor, most teachers—and the principals who supervise their classes—operate as if progressive education had not proved the case for noise and freedom of bodily motion. (Dewey stresses the salutary alternation of boisterousness and tranquility.) The seats are no longer bolted to the floor, but they still face front. Of course, the classes are too large to cope with without "discipline." Then make them smaller, or don't wonder if children escape out of the cage, either into truancy or baffled daydream. Here is a typical case: an architect replacing a Harlem school is forbidden by the Board to spend money on soundproofing the classrooms, even though the principal has called it a necessity for the therapy of pent-up and resentful children. The resentment, pent-up hostility, is a major cause of reactive stupidity; yet there is usually an absolute ban on overt expression of hostility, or even of normal anger and aggression.

Again, one has to be blind not to see that, from the onset of puberty, the dissidence from school is importantly sexual. Theoretically, the junior high school was introduced to fit this change of life; yet astoundingly, it is sexless. My own view, for what it's worth, is that sexuality is lovely, there cannot be too much of it, it is self-limiting if it is satisfactory, and satisfaction diminishes tension and clears the mind for attention and learning. Therefore, sexual expression should be approved in and out of season, also in school, and where necessary made the subject of instruction. But whether or not this view is correct, it certainly is more practical than the apparent attempt of the schools to operate as if sexual drives simply did not exist. When, on so crucial an issue, the schools act a hundred years out of date, they are crucially irrelevant.

But the following *is* something new:

> Trenton, May 24 (AP)—A state health official believes some overanxious New Jersey parents are dosing their children with tranquilizers before sending them to school...the Health Department pediatrician assigned to the State Education Department said the parents apparently are trying to protect the children from cracking under pressure for good grades.

(d) Terrible damage is done to children simply by the size and standardization of the big system. Suppose a class size of 20 is good for average purposes; it does *not* follow that 35 is better than nothing. Rather, it is likely to be positively harmful, because the children have ceased to be persons and the teacher is destroyed as a teacher. A teacher with a 10-year-old class reading at 7-year level will have to use the content as well as the vocabulary of *Dick and Jane* since that is the text-book bought by the hundred thousands. The experience of a wise principal is that the most essential part of his job is to know every child's name and be an available "good father," so he wants a school for 400. Yet the city will build the school for 2000, because only that is practical, even though the essence is entirely dissipated. The chief part of learning is in the community of scholars, where classwork and social life may cohere; yet social engineers like Dr. Conant will, for putative efficiencies, centralize the high schools—the "enriched" curriculum with equipment is necessary for the national needs.

A program—e.g., to prevent drop-out—will be, by an attentive teacher, exquisitely tailored to the children he works with; he will have a success. Therefore his program must be standardized, watered down, for 75 schools—otherwise it cannot be financed—although now it is worthless. But here is an unbeatable anecdote: An architect is employed to replace a dilapidated school but is forbidden to consult the principal and teachers of the school about their needs, since his building must conform to uniform plans at headquarters, the plans being two generations out of date. As a functionalist, the architect demurs, and it required an *ad hoc* assembly of all the superintendents to give him special permission.

Presumably all this is administratively necessary, but then it is also necessary for bruised children to quit. Our society makes a persistent error in metaphysics. We are so mesmerized by the operation of a system with the appropriate name, for instance, "Education," that we assume that it *must* be working somewhat, though admittedly not perfectly, when perhaps it has ceased to fulfill its function altogether and might even be preventing the function, for instance, education.

(e) Especially today, when the hours of work will sharply diminish, the schools are supposed to educate for the satisfaction of life and for the worthwhile use of leisure. Again, let us try to be realistic, as a youngster is. For most people, I think, a candid self-examination will show that their most absorbing, long, and satisfactory hours are spent in activities like friendly competitive sports, gambling, looking for love and lovemaking, earnest or argumentative conversation, political action with signs and sit-ins, solitary study and reading, contemplation of nature and cosmos, arts and crafts, music, and religion. Now none of these requires much money. Indeed, elaborate equipment takes the heart out of them. Friends use one another as resources. God, nature, and creativity are free. The media of the fine arts are cheap stuff. Health, luck, and affection are the only requirements for good sex. Good food requires taking pains more than spending money.

What is the moral for our purposes? Can it be denied that in some respects the drop-outs make a wiser choice than many who go to school, not to get real goods but to get money? Their choice of the "immediate"—their notorious "inability to tolerate delay"—is not altogether impulsive and neurotic. The bother is that in our present culture, which puts its entire emphasis on the consumption of expensive commodities, they are so nagged by inferiority, exclusion, and despair of the future that they cannot enjoy their leisure with a good conscience. Because they know little, they are deprived of many profound simple satisfactions and they never know what to do with themselves. Being afraid of exposing themselves to awkwardness and ridicule, they just hang around. And our urban social arrangements—e.g., high rent—have made it impossible for anybody to be decently poor on a "low" standard. One is either in the rat-race or has dropped out of society altogether.

(f) As a loyal academic, I must make a further observation. Mainly to provide Ph.D.'s, there is at present an overwhelming pressure to gear the "better" elementary schools to the graduate-universities. This is the great current reform, genre of Rickover. But what if the top of the ladder is corrupt and corrupts the lower grades? On visits to 70 colleges everywhere in the country, I have been appalled at how rarely the subjects are studied in a right academic spirit, for their truth and beauty and as part of humane international culture. The students are given, and seek, a narrow expertise, "mastery," aimed at licenses and salary. They are indoctrinated with a national thoughtlessness that is not even chauvinistic. Administrators sacrifice the community of scholars to aggrandizement and extramurally sponsored research.

Conversely, there is almost never conveyed the sense in which learning is truly practical, to enlighten experience, give courage to initate and change, reform the state, deepen personal and social peace. On the contrary, the entire educational system itself creates professional cynicism or the resigned conviction that Nothing Can Be Done. If this is the University, how can we hope for aspiring scholarship in the elementary schools? On the contrary, everything will be grades and conforming, getting ahead not in the subject of interest but up the ladder. Students "do" Bronx Science in order to "make" M.I.T. and they "do" M.I.T. in order to "make" Westinghouse; some of them have "done" Westinghouse in order to "make" jail.

vi

What then? The compulsory system has become a universal trap, and it is no good. Very many of the youth, both poor and middle class, might be better off if the system simply did not exist, even if they then had no formal schooling at all. (I am extremely curious for a philosophic study of Prince Edward County in Virginia, where for some years schooling did not exist for Negro children.)

But what would become of these children? For very many, both poor and middle class, their homes are worse than the schools, and the city streets are worse in another way. Our urban and suburban environments are precisely not cities or communities where adults naturally attend to the young and educate to a viable life. Also, perhaps especially in the case of the overt drop-outs, the state of their body and soul is such that we must give them refuge and remedy, whether it be called school, settlement house, youth worker, or work camp.

There are thinkable alternatives. As occasion arises, I shall offer alternative proposals that I as a single individual have heard of or thought up. Here are half a dozen directly relevant to the subject we have been discussing, the system as compulsory trap. In principle, when a law begins to do more harm than good, the best policy is to alleviate it or try doing without it.

i. Have "no school at all" for a few classes. These children should be selected from tolerable, though not necessarily cultured, homes. They should be neighbors and numerous enough to be a society for one another and so that they do not feel merely "different." Will they learn the rudiments anyway? This experiment cannot do the children any academic harm, since there is good evidence that normal children will make up the first seven years school-work with four to seven months of good teaching.

ii. Dispense with the school building for a few classes; provide teachers and use the city itself as the school—its streets, cafeterias, stores, movies, museums, parks, and factories. Where feasible, it certainly makes more sense to teach using the real subject-matter than to bring an abstraction of the subject-matter into the school-building as "curriculum." Such a class should probably not exceed 10 children for one pedagogue. The idea—it is the model of Athenian education—is not dissimilar to Youth gang work, but not applied to delinquents and not playing to the gang ideology.

iii. Along the same lines, but both outside and inside the school building, use appropriate *unlicensed* adults of the community—the druggist, the storekeeper, the mechanic—as the proper educators of the young into the grown-up world. By this means we can try to overcome the separation of the young from the grown-up world so characteristic in modern urban life, and to diminish the omnivorous authority of the professional school-people. Certainly it would be a useful and animating experience for the adults. (There is the beginning of such a volunteer program in the New York and some other systems.)

iv. Make class attendance not compulsory, in the manner of A. S. Neill's *Summerhill*. If the teachers are good, absence would tend to be eliminated; if they are bad, let them know it. The compulsory law is useful to get the children away from the parents, but it must not result in trapping the children. A fine modification of this suggestion is the rule used by Frank Brown in Florida: he permits the children to be absent for a week or a month to engage in any worthwhile enterprise or visit any new environment.

v. Decentralize an urban school (or do not build a new big building) into small units, 20 to 50, in available store-fronts or clubhouses. These tiny schools equipped with record-player and pin-ball machine, could combine play, socializing, discussion, and formal teaching. For special events, the small units can be brought together into a common auditorium or gymnasium, so as to give the sense of the greater community. Correspondingly, I think it would be worthwhile to give the Little Red Schoolhouse a spin under modern urban conditions, and see how it works out: that is, to combine all the ages in a little room for 25 to 30, rather than to grade by age.

vi. Use a pro rata part of the school money to send children to economically marginal farms for a couple of months of the year, perhaps 6 children from mixed backgrounds to a farmer. The only requirement is that the farmer feed them and not beat them; best, of course, if they take part in the farm work. This will give the farmer cash, as part of the generally desirable program to redress the urban-rural ratio to something nearer to 70% to 30%. (At present, less than 8% of families are rural.) Conceivably, some of the urban children will take to the other way of life, and we might generate a new kind of rural culture.

I frequently suggest these and similar proposals at teachers colleges, and I am looked at with an eerie look—do I really mean to *diminish* the state-aid grant for each student-day? But mostly the objective is that such proposals entail intolerable administrative difficulties.

Above all, we must apply these or any other proposals to particular individuals and small groups, without the obligation of uniformity. There is a case for uniform standards of achievement, lodged in the Regents, but they *cannot* be reached by uniform techniques. The claim that standardization of procedure is more efficient, less costly, or alone administratively practical, is often false. Particular inventiveness requires thought, but thought does not cost money.

ROBERT M. HUTCHINS

Robert M. Hutchins was born in Brooklyn, New York, on January 17, 1899. His father taught theology at Oberlin College which Hutchins attended for a few years. But his education was interrupted by World War I. During the war he served as an ambulance driver in Italy. After the war he went to Yale where he received a B.A. degree in 1921.

After teaching English and history for two years he returned to Yale to study law and received his L.L.B. degree in 1925. He was professor of law at Yale from 1923 to 1929 and dean of the law school from 1928 to 1929.

Hutchins left Yale in 1929 to become president of the University of Chicago at 30. He remained as president until 1945 and then as chancellor until 1951.

As president of Chicago, Hutchins reorganized the university's administrative system and inaugurated the Chicago plan of a four year junior college and a liberal arts university which were independent of the professional schools.

Hutchins left Chicago and became associate director of the Ford Foundation in 1951, editor of the *Great Books of the Western World* in 1952, and president of the Fund for the Republic in 1954. He remained with the Fund for the Republic until 1961, after which time he became president of the Center for the Study of Democratic Institutions at Santa Barbara, California.

Hutchins has written a number of books on education, including *The Higher Learning in America, Education for Freedom, The Conflict in Education in a Democratic Society, Morals, Religion and Higher Education, Some Observations on American Education, The University of Utopia,* and *The Learning Society.*

Hutchins believes that we are becoming too specialized in our approach toward education and that we need more of a grounding in the liberal arts. He advocates that the entire educational system orient itself to an integrated plan of liberal education, to be primarily concerned with the intellect. Hutchins feels that our schools should promote a search for truth, God, and morality. Like Mortimer Adler, Hutchins is greatly in favor of a "Great Books" approach to education as a way of providing a basis for a liberal education.

THE CONFLICT IN EDUCATION

Robert M. Hutchins

If the public, the teachers, and the professors all understood the educational system, we could develop a tradition in this country that would be far more effective in giving us the kind of education we need than laws, witch-hunts, or regulations that teachers must subscribe to oaths that, as Governor Warren of California has said, any traitor would take with a laugh. On the side of the teachers and professors, the professional tradition would mean that they taught responsibly. On the side of the public the tradition would mean that the public restrained itself in the exercise of its legal control.

Because I am concerned with the development of this tradition I deplore every futile, childish, and irrelevant activity in which the educational system engages. Educators do things that the public wants in order to get the support of the public. They do little to explain to the public why it should not want the things it does. I like intercollegiate football, but I recommended its abolition at Chicago, because the game in its industrial, big-time form has nothing to do with education and yet has the effect of diverting everybody's attention from the educational problems with which universities should be wrestling. So I deplore the multiplication of trivial courses, in cosmetology, fishing and tap-dancing, which swell the catalogues of great American universities and which have no purpose except to help the student wile away four years without using his mind. Think of the most futile, childish, irrelevant subject you can—think of parlor games, think of self-beautifica-

---

(Pp. 12-20) "Adjustment to the Environment" from *The Conflict in Education* by Robert M. Hutchins. Copyright, 1953 by Harper & Row, Publishers, Inc. Reprinted by permission of Harper & Row, Publishers, Inc.

tion, think of anything you like—I will undertake to find it for you among the courses offered by American institutions of higher learning.

I had no sooner written these words than *Life* magazine came along to prove my point by announcing that at an American university it is possible to get college credit for being a clown, something that even I, after decades of disillusionment, could never have thought of. *Life* concludes its account with words that might well be the epitaph of the higher learning in America: the students, says *Life*, regard this work "as just part of a normal liberal education." I need say no more to show that neither the public nor the educational profession has a clear conception of education. They have no standard by which to judge what belongs in education and what does not.

What belongs in education is what helps the student to learn to think for himself, to form an independent judgment, and to take his part as a responsible citizen. Although I will admit that in the hands of Socrates any subject can be made important, even clowning, because any subject can lead to important questions, there was only one Socrates, and I know of none in any educational system today. We have to frame the course of study of American schools, colleges, and universities in the light of the capacity of ordinary teachers. If the object of the educational system is to help young people learn to think for themselves, it should help them to think about the most important subjects, and these are discussed in the greatest works of the greatest writers of the past and present. To destroy the Western tradition of independent thought it is not necessary to burn the books. All we have to do is to leave them unread for a couple of generations.

In the United States little effort is made to raise the level of mass cultivation through the schools. The leading theories or doctrines of education say nothing on this subject.

The first of these doctrines is the theory of adjustment. Here the object is to fit the student into his physical, social, political, economic, and intellectual environment with a minimum of discomfort to the society. Freud took the view that the object of education was to make young people healthy and efficient, to adapt them to their surroundings, to make them successful in the terms of the society in which they were brought up. His summary is: "I should go so far as to say that revolutionary children are not desirable from any point of view." This caution seems unnecessary; for no society would tolerate a revolutionary educational system.

So T. S. Eliot seems to give his powerful sanction to an educational program that adapts the child to the political organization under which he is to live.

So the chief aim of the program of UNESCO in fundamental education, which is the principal program of the organization, is to enable the peoples of underdeveloped countries "to adjust themselves to their changing environment."

In America the doctrine of adjustment is perhaps the leading theory. Here it results from a misconception of John Dewey. Since he is not a clear writer, his followers may perhaps be excused for their failure to notice that when he talked about adjustment to the environment, he meant that the environment should first be improved. Dewey was essentially a social reformer, and it is tragic that he should have laid the foundation for the proposition that the aim of education is to adjust the young to their environment, good or bad.

The theory of adjustment or adaptation was carried to its logical extreme in a women's college in America, which based its curriculum on a job analysis of the diaries of 323 mature women. The categories of the activities of these women constitute the structure of the curriculum, without regard to whether or not mature women ought to do or are now doing when this poll was taken.

Thus it will be seen that the theory of adjustment leads to a curriculum of miscellaneous dead facts. The way to adjust to the environment is to learn the facts about the environment. Since it is impossible to tell what the environment will be, the student can only be informed about the environment that exists while he is in school. But all that is known with certainty about the environment is that it will be different by the time the student has to adjust himself to it.

The doctrine of adjustment or adaptation is not well adapted to America. America is, and always has been, a society in transition. Seventy million Americans live in a different house today from the one they occupied ten years ago. America is the example par excellence of the rapidity of technological change. Vocations employing thousands of men may be wiped out overnight and be replaced by others that were not thought of the day before.

One of the most popular courses in the American schools is stenography. Think of the havoc that will be wrought if the dictating machine becomes the standard method of conducting office correspondence. A great American university has established a school of what is called cosmetology, announcing that what it called the profession of beautician "is the fastest growing in this state." Think what will happen to the graduates of this educational institution if self-beautification for ladies becomes as simple a matter as it is for men.

America is probably the easiest place to earn a living in the world. Yet more emphasis is placed on vocational training in the American schools than in any others. There are many reasons for this; but the one I wish to mention now is an example of the proposition that what is honored in a country will be cultivated there. We must admit that what is honored in America is material success. All you have to do to understand this is to compare the position of intellectuals and artists in America with their position in Europe. The model American is the successful businessman. Artists and intellectuals are regarded in the light of charity patients or excess baggage. Consequently the attention of the American is drawn at an early date to the necessity of adjusting himself to his economic environment in such a way that he will be successful.

I shall attempt in a moment a general critique of the doctrine of adjustment or adaptation. Here I wish to mention one or two consequences of that branch of the doctrine which deals with economic or vocational adjustment. The question it raises is this: assuming that the young must adjust to their environment, including their economic environment, can the educational system manage, supervise, and direct the whole job? In particular, can the educational system give a boy as good a training for a particular task in industry as the industry itself could give him? In America technical institutes of the European type are virtually unknown. Vocational training is given along with all other types of training in the same schools. Because of the relative ease of vocational instruction and because of the immediate interest it excites on the part of the pupil, such instruction has the tendency to force out of the course of study any other kind of instruction. Yet we learned in the war that the airplane companies could produce in a few weeks better airplane mechanics than the schools could produce in years. The pupils in the schools were necessarily trained by obsolescent teachers with obsolescent machinery. Hence the result of the emphasis on vocational training in America is poor mechanics without education.

America is not only the easiest place to earn a living in the world; it is also the place with the most leisure in the world. The average industrial worker in America gets more than fifty dollars for a forty-hour week. He now works twenty hours a week less than he did forty years ago. At the same time that industrial operations have been simplified to the point where little or no training is required for them—they can in fact be performed by twelve-year-old children—unprecedented leisure has opened before the American citizen. Still one of the principal aims of the educational system is to educate the citizen to work for a living. It does not educate him at all in the right use of his leisure.

The new found leisure of the American is therefore spent in relaxation, and that provided by the tavern and the television set is almost equally demoralizing. The prospect that television opens before us in America, with nobody speaking and nobody reading, suggests that a bleak and torpid epoch may lie ahead in which the population will eventually sink, in accordance with the principles of evolution, to the level of the lowest forms of vegetable life.

Scientists of the University of Chicago have lately detected something that looks like moss growing on the planet Mars. Perhaps Mars was once inhabited by beings like ourselves, who had the misfortune, some millions of years ago, to invent television. The twin aims that have animated mankind since the dawn of history, the conquest of nature and relief from drudgery, now almost accomplished in America, have ended in the trivialization of our lives.

There are, of course, many reasons for this; but one of them surely is that our educational system has given us no resources that we can employ to give our leisure time significance. When we are not working, all we can do is to amuse ourselves. The deep and permanent melancholia that underlies the American temperament must be ascribed, in part at least, to the boredom that the perpetual search for amusement at length induces.

The whole doctrine of adjustment to the environment seems to me radically erroneous. As I have said, it leads to a curriculum of miscellaneous dead facts. It leads to vocational training, which the schools are not equipped to give and which misses the most important contribution that the schools can make. But it is far more urgent that we notice that our mission here on earth is to change our environment, not to adjust ourselves to it. If we become maladjusted in the process, so much the worse for the environment. The message that UNESCO should carry to the people of backward countries is not that they should adjust themselves to their changing environment, but that they should change their environment.

* * *

The obvious failures of the doctrines of adaptation, immediate needs, social reform, and of the doctrine that we need no doctrine at all may suggest to us that we require a better definition of education. Let us concede that every society must have some system that attempts to adapt the young to their social and political environment. If the society is bad, in the sense, for example, in which the Nazi state was bad, the system will aim at the same bad ends. To the extent that it makes man bad in order that they may be tractable subjects of a bad state, the system may help to achieve the social ideals of the society. It may be what the society wants; it may even be what the society needs, if it is to perpetuate its form and accomplish its aims. In pragmatic terms, in terms of success in the society, it may be a "good" system.

But it seems to me clearer to say that, though it may be a system of training, or instruction, or adaptation, or meeting immediate needs, it is not a system of education. It seems clearer to say that the purpose of education is to improve men. Any system that tries to make them bad is not education, but something else. If, for example, democracy is the best form of society, a system that adapts the young to it will be an educational system. If despotism is a bad form of society, a system that adapts the young to it will not be an educational system, and the better it succeeds in adapting them the less educational it will be.

Every man has a function as a man. The function of a citizen or a subject may vary from society to society, and the system of training, or adaptation, or instruction, or meeting immediate needs may vary with it. But the function of a man as man is the same in every age and in every society, since it results from his nature as a man. The aim of an educational system is the same in every age and in every society where such a system can exist: it is to improve man as man.

If we are going to talk about improving men and societies, we have to believe that there is some difference between good and bad. This difference must not be, as the positivists think it is, merely conventional. We cannot tell this difference by any examination of the effectiveness of a given program as the pragmatists propose; the time required to estimate these effects is usually too long and the complexity of society is always too great for us to say that the consequences of a given program are altogether clear. We cannot discover the difference between good and bad by going to the laboratory, for men and societies are not laboratory animals. If we believe that there is no truth, there is no knowledge, and there are no values except those which are validated by laboratory experiment, we cannot talk about the improvement of men and societies, for we can have no standard of judging anything that takes place among men or in societies.

Society is to be improved not by forcing a program of social reform down its throat, through the schools or otherwise, but by the improvement of the individuals who compose it. As Plato said, "Governments reflect human nature. States are not made out of stone or wood, but out of the characters of their citizens: these turn the scale and draw everything after them." The individual is the heart of society.

To talk about making men better we must have some idea of what men are, because if we have none, we can have no idea of what is good or bad for them. If men are brutes like other animals, then there is no reason why they should not be treated like brutes by anybody who can gain power over them. And there is no reason why they should not be trained as brutes are trained. A sound philosophy in general suggests that men are rational, moral, and spiritual beings and that the improvement of men means the fullest development of their rational, moral, and spiritual powers. All men have these powers, and all men should develop them to the fullest extent.

Man is by nature free, and he is by nature social. To use his freedom rightly he needs discipline. To live in society he needs the moral virtues. Good moral and intellectual habits are required for the fullest development of the nature of man.

To develop fully as a social, political animal, man needs participation in his own government. A benevolent despotism will not do. You cannot expect the slave to show the virtues of the free man unless you first set him free. Only democracy in which all men rule and are ruled in turn for the good life of the whole community, can be an absolutely good form of government.

The community rests on the social nature of men. It requires communication among its members. They do not have to agree with one another; but they must be able to understand one another. And their philosophy in general must supply them with a common purpose and a common concept of man and society adequate to hold the community together. Civilization is the deliberate pursuit of a common ideal. The good society is not just a society we happen to like or to be used to. It is a community of good men.

Education deals with the development of the intellectual powers of men. Their moral and spiritual powers are the sphere of the family and the church. All three agencies must work in harmony; for, though a man has three aspects, he is still one man. But the schools cannot take over the role of the family and the church without promoting the atrophy of those institutions and failing in the task that is proper to the schools.

We cannot talk about the intellectual powers of men, though we can talk about training them, or amusing them, or adapting them, and meeting their immediate needs, unless our philosophy in general tells us that there is knowledge and that there is a difference between true and false. We must believe, too, that there are other means of obtaining knowledge than scientific experimentation. If knowledge can be sought only in the laboratory, many fields in which we thought we had knowledge will offer us nothing but opinion or superstition, and we shall be forced to conclude that we cannot know anything about the most important aspects of man and society. If we are to set about developing the intellecutal powers of men through having them acquire knowledge of the most important subjects, we have to begin with the proposition that experimentation and empirical data will be of only limited use to us, contrary to the convictions of many American social scientists, and that philosophy, history, literature, and art give us knowledge, and significant knowledge, on the most significant issues.

If the object of education is the improvement of men, then any system of education that is without values is a contradiction in terms. A system that seeks bad values is bad. A system that denies the existence of value denies the possibility of education. Relativism, scientism, skepticism, and anti-intellectualism, the four horsemen of the philosophical apocalypse, have produced that chaos in education which will end in the disintegration of the West.

The prime object of education is to know what is good for man. It is to know the goods in their order. There is a hierarchy of values. The task of education is to help us understand it, establish it, and live by it. This, Aristotle had in mind when he said: "It is not the possessions but the desires of men that must be equalized, and this is impossible unless they have a sufficient education according to the nature of things."

Such an education is far removed from the triviality of that produced by the doctrines of adaptation, of immediate needs, of social reform, or of the doctrine of no doctrine at all. Such an education will not adapt the young to a bad environment, but it will encourage them to make it good. It will not overlook immediate needs, but it will place these needs in their proper relationship to more distant, less tangible, and more important goods. It will be the only effective means of reforming society. *(whose society do they want to reform? theirs or others?)*

This is the education appropriate to free men. It is liberal education. If all men are to be free, all men must have this education. It makes no difference how they are to earn their living or what their special interests or aptitudes may be. They can learn to make a living, and they can develop their special interests and aptitudes, after they have laid the foundation of free and responsible manhood through liberal education. It will not do to say that they are incapable of such education. This claim is made by those who are too indolent or unconvinced to make the effort to give such education to the masses.

Nor will it do to say that there is not enough time to give everybody a liberal education before he becomes a specialist. In America, at least, the waste and frivolity of the educational system are so great that it would be possible through getting rid of them to give every citizen a liberal education and make him a qualified specialist, too, in less time than is now consumed in turning out uneducated specialists.

A liberal education aims to develop the powers of understanding and judgment. It is impossible that too many people can be educated in this sense, because there cannot be too many people with understanding and judgment. We hear a great deal today about the dangers that will come upon us through the frustration of educated people who have got educated in the expectation that education will get them a better job, and who then fail to get it. But surely this depends on the representations that are made to the young about what education is. If we allow them to believe that education will get them better jobs and encourage them to get educated with this end in view, they are entitled to a sense of frustration if, when they have got the education, they do not get the jobs. But, if we say that they should be educated in order to be men, and that everybody, whether he is a ditch-digger or a bank president, should have this education because he is a man, then the ditch-digger may still feel frustrated, but not because of his education.

Nor is it possible for a person to have too much liberal education, because it is impossible to have too much understanding and judgment. But it is possible to undertake too much in the name of liberal education

89

in youth. The object of liberal education in youth is not to teach the young all they will ever need to know. It is to give them the habits, ideas, and techniques that they need to continue to educate themselves. Thus the object of formal institutional liberal education in youth is to prepare the young to educate themselves throughout their lives.

I would remind you of the impossibility of learning to understand and judge many of the most important things in youth. The judgment and understanding of practical affairs can amount to little in the absence of experience with practical affairs. Subjects that cannot be understood without experience should not be taught to those who are without experience. Or, if these subjects are taught to those who are without experience, it should be clear that these subjects can be taught only by way of introduction and that their value to the student depends on his continuing to study them as he acquires experience. The tragedy in America is that economics, ethics, politics, history, and literature are studied in youth, and seldom studied again. Therefore the graduates of American universities seldom understand them.

This pedagogical principle, that subjects requiring experience can be learned only by the experiences, leads to the conclusion that the most important branch of education is the education of adults. We sometimes seem to think of education as something like the mumps, measles, whooping-cough, or chicken-pox. If a person has had education in childhood, he need not, in fact he cannot, have it again. But the pedagogical principle that the most important things can be learned only in mature life is supported by a sound philosophy in general. Men are rational animals. They achieve their terrestrial felicity by the use of reason. And this means that they have to use it for their entire lives. To say that they should learn only in childhood would mean that they were human only in childhood.

And it would mean that they were unfit to be citizens of a republic.[1] A republic, a true *res publica*, can maintain justice, peace, freedom, and order only by the exercise of intelligence. When we speak of the consent of the governed, we mean, since men are not angels who seek the truth intuitively and do not have to learn it, that every act of assent on the part of the governed is a product of learning. A republic is really a common educational life in process. So Montesquieu said that,

---

[1] I owe this discussion to the suggestions of Scott Buchanan.

whereas the principle of a monarchy was honor, and the principle of a tyranny was fear, the principle of a republic was education.

Hence the ideal republic is the republic of learning. It is the Utopia by which all actual political republics are measured. The goal toward which we started with the Athenians twenty-five centuries ago is an unlimited republic of learning and a world-wide political republic mutually supporting each other.

All men are capable of learning. Learning does not stop as long as a man lives, unless his learning power atrophies because he does not use it. Political freedom cannot endure unless it is accompanied by provision for the unlimited acquisition of knowledge. Truth is not long retained in human affairs without continual learning and relearning. Peace is unlikely unless there are continuous, unlimited opportunities for learning and unless men continuously avail themselves of them. The world of law and justice for which we yearn, the world-wide political republic, cannot be realized without the world-wide republic of learning. The civilization we seek will be achieved when all men are citizens of the world republic of law and justice and of the republic of learning all their lives long.

ALDOUS HUXLEY

Aldous Huxley was born on July 26, 1894, at Godalming, Surrey, England. He was the grandson of Thomas Henry Huxley, the famous scientist.

Huxley was educated at Eton and at Balliol College, Oxford. He taught for a while at Eton, but soon decided to devote himself to writing. Huxley traveled widely, and spent much of his time in the 1920's in France and Italy. He is known as a writer of essays, biography, drama, and verse. Some of his most notable works, many of which have implications for education are *Point Counter Point, Brave New World, The Perennial Philosophy, Ape and Essence, The Doors of Perception, Proper Studies, Tomorrow and Tomorrow and Tomorrow.*

Huxley believes that Dewey had many useful ideas, but that they have been corrupted and misstated by his followers. He disapproves very strongly of our intent to educate everyone in what he feels is the same way, and believes that education as we know it today is primarily for conformity and business success.

Huxley feels that at the present time we are pursuing technological advancement without a corresponding advancement in wisdom. He states that he would like to see a more humanistic attitude in our present educational practices, and believes that we also need more freedom of thought and freedom from psychological restraints. Huxley feels that we have failed to make the best of what we have, and man born a "sub-man" is often condemned by our present educational system to spend his life as a "sub-sub man."

TOMORROW AND TOMORROW AND TOMORROW

Aldous Huxley

Too much theorizing, as we all know, is fatal to the soul. Too many lectures will cause the green tree to wither, will turn its golden fruits to dust. Life flows back into us when we turn from the stale oldness of theological notions to the newness of spiritual experience; when we exchange the learn'd astronomers' proofs and figures for nocturnal silence and the stars. St. Paul and the poets are talking about some of the most obvious facts of experience. But these facts are not the only facts. Theory is gray and diagrams have no nourishment in them. And yet without scientific theories, without philosophy and theology and law, we should be nothing but Yahoos. The letter condemns us to spiritual death; but the absence of the letter condemns us to something just as bad. Whether we like it or not, we are amphibians, living simultaneously in the world of experience and the world of nations, in the world of direct apprehension of Nature, God and ourselves, and the world of abstract, verbalized knowledge about these primary facts. Our business as human beings is to make the best of both these worlds.

Unfortunately, organized education has done very little, hitherto, to help us in this task. For organized education is predominantly verbal education. In the Middle Ages the liberal arts were seven in number. The first three—grammar, logic and rhetoric—concerned themselves with the language of common speech, philosophy and literature respectively. The fourth, arithmetic, was the art of handling the special language of numbers. Geometry was the fifth art, and included natural history; but this natural history was studied almost exclusively in encyclopedias composed by men who had studied it in other encyclopedias. The sixth of the liberal arts was astronomy; and its study entailed some observation of the non-verbal universe. In music, the seventh and last of the arts, a non-verbal aspect of the human mind was studied. (We should remember, however, that medieval educators always treated music as a science, and concerned themselves hardly at all with music as a mode of expression, a source of pleasure or of insight.)

In modern practice a course in liberal arts is less overwhelmingly verbal than it was in the past. Words are still the medium in which teachers and pupils carry on most of their activities. But they are not the only medium. Modern education provides for numerous excursions into external fact and even into that given inner world, in which the non-verbal side of our amphibious nature has its being. Students are now required to observe non-verbal facts and make experiments with them; they are encouraged to cultivate their artistic skills, to refine their tastes and sharpen their sensibilities. All this is greatly to the good. But it is not yet enough. We must do more for the non-verbal part of our amphibious nature, we must do better, than we are doing now.

Exponents of Progressive Education probably think that they are already doing everything that can be done. Under the influence of John Dewey, they have stressed the importance of non-verbal activity as a means of learning. History, for example, is now often taught in a series of "projects." Stonehenge is reconstructed with brickbats in the back yard. Life in the Middle Ages is dramatically reproduced—minus, of course, the dirt, the violence and the theology, which were the essence of that life. Whether children learn more through these mud-pie techniques of education than they would learn by being shown pictures and reading an intelligent book, I do not profess to know. The important point, in our present context, is that the "doing," through which the children are supposed to learn, is left unanalyzed by the Progressive Educators who advocate it. So far as they are concerned, doing is doing; there is nothing to choose between one kind of doing and another. John Dewey himself knew better; but his followers have chosen to ignore his qualifications of the learning-by-doing doctrine and to plunge headlong and with unquestioning enthusiasm into their mud pies.

But before I pursue this subject any further, let me return for a moment to our amphibian. To my earlier list of man's double lives I would like to add yet another item. Every human being is a conscious self; but, below the threshold of consciousness, every human being is also a not-self—or, more precisely, he is five or six merging but clearly distinguishable not-selves. There is, first of all, the personal, home-made not-self—the not-self of habits and conditioned reflexes, the not-self of buried-alive reactions to remote events and forgotten words, the not-self of fossil infancy and the festering remains of a past that refuses to die. This personal not-self is that region of the subconscious with which psychiatry mainly deals. Next comes the not-self that used to be called the vegetative soul or the entelechy. This is the not-self in charge of the body—the not-self who, when we wish to walk, actually does the walking, the not-self that controls our breathing, our heartbeat, our glandular secretion; the not-self that is prepared to digest even dough-nuts; the not-self that heals wounds and brings us back to health when we have been ill. Next, there is the not-self who inhabits the world from which we derive our insights and inspirations. This is the not-self who spoke to Socrates through his daimon, who dreamed the text of *Kubla Kahn*, who dictated *King Lear* and the *Agamemnon* and the *Tibetan Book of the Dead*, the not-self who is responsible in all of us for every enhancement of wisdom, every sudden accession of vital or intellectual power. Beyond this world of inspiration lies the world of what Jung has called the Archetypes—those great shared symbols which stand for man's deepest tendencies, his perennial conflicts and ubiquitous problems. Next comes the world of visionary experience, where a mysterious not-self lives in the midst, not of shared human symbols, but of shared non-human facts—facts from which the theologians of the various religions have derived their notions of the Other World, of Heaven and Hell. And finally, beyond all the rest, but immanent in every mental or material event, is that universal Not-Self, which men have called the Holy Spirit, the Atman-Brahman, the Clear Light, Suchness.

A self can affect and be affected by its associated not-selves in many different ways. Here for example is a conscious self which responds inappropriately to circumstances. In the process it is apt to fill the personal not-self with all manner of fears, greeds, hates and wrong judgments. Thus distorted, the personal not-self reacts upon the conscious self, forcing it to behave even more inappropriately than before. And so the game goes on, each party contributing to the delinquency of the other. Self and personal not-self have set up a mutual deterioration society.

For the not-self in charge of bodily functions the consequences of this are disastrous. Left to its own devices, this physiological intelligence is almost incapable of making a mistake. Interfered with by a delinquent ego and an insane personal subconscious, it loses its native infallibility, and the organism at once falls prey to psychosomatic disease. Health is a state of harmony between conscious self, personal not-self and vegetative soul.

The last three not-selves constitute the very essence of our being, and yet are so transcendently other as to be beyond our power to affect them. The ego and the personal not-self can poison one another and play havoc with the vegetative soul. They can do nothing to hurt the indwelling Spirit. What they can do, what for most people, most of the time, they actually succeed in doing, is to eclipse these inner lights. They set up a more or less completely opaque screen between our consciousness and the transcendental not-selves with which every self is associated. What is called Enlightenment is simply the removal of this eclipsing barrier.

The foregoing account of man's double life as a self associated with a group of not-selves has been, of necessity, very brief and schematic. But I hope, none the less, that it may serve to illuminate our problem: How can we educate the psycho-physical instrument, by means of which we learn and live?

The psycho-physical instrument is one and indivisible; but for practical purposes we may regard it as being made up of several distinct components. Accordingly, the curriculum of our hypothetical course in what may be called the non-verbal humanities will include the following items. Training of the kinesthetic sense. Training of the special sense. Training of memory. Training in control of the autonomic nervous system. Training for spiritual insight.

The most fundamental of our awarenesses is the kinesthetic sense. This is the sense which registers muscular tension within the body, and which tells us about the changes in muscular tension that accompany physical movement and variations in our mental state. The kinesthetic sense is the main line of communication between the conscious self and the personal subconscious on the one hand and the vegetative soul on the other. When this sense is debauched—and in our urban-industrial civilization it seems to get debauched very easily—two things happen. First, the individual develops a habit of using his psycho-physical instrument improperly. And, second, he loses his sense of what we may call muscular morality, his basic standard of physical right and wrong. Habit is second nature; and when we have gone on doing an unnatural thing long enough, it comes, by mere familiarity, to seem completely right and proper. What is needed, at this basic level of psycho-physical education, is some way of unlearning our habits of improper use, some method by which the debauched kinesthetic sense may be restored to its pristine integrity.

Such a method exists. It has been developed in more than fifty years of experimentation and teaching by Mr. F. M. Alexander, an Australian by birth who has worked for most of his long life in England and the United States.[1] The importance of Alexander's work was early recognized by John Dewey, who contributed valuable prefaces to three of his books. Alexander's fundamental discovery (since confirmed by physiologists and zoologists working in other fields) is that there are, in Dewey's words, "certain basic, central organic habits and attitudes, which condition *every* act we perform, every use we make of ourselves." When we lose these natural good habits and impose upon ourselves improper habits of use, everything goes wrong, not merely in the body, but also (insofar as physical events condition mental events) in the mind. The degree of wrongness may be great or small; but since all bad habits tend to become worse with time, it is in the highest degree desirable that they should be corrected at the earliest opportunity. Alexander's technique, writes John Dewey, "gives the educator a standard of psycho-physical health—in which what we call morality is included. It also supplies the means whereby that standard may be progressively and endlessly achieved. It provides therefore the conditions for the central direction of all educational processes. It bears the same relation to education that education itself bears to all other human activities." These are strong words; for Dewey was convinced that man's only hope lay in education. But just as education is absolutely necessary to the world at large, so Alexander's methods of training the psycho-physical instrument are absolutely necessary to education. Schooling without proper training of the psycho-physical instrument cannot, in the very nature of things, do more than a limited amount of good, do the child a great deal of harm by systematically ingraining his habits of improper use. Learning by doing is a sound principle only if the doing is good doing. If it is bad doing (and in the vast majority of cases it IS bad) learning by doing is hopelessly unsound.

---

[1] For details of Alexander's educational methods the reader is referred to his four books: *Man's Supreme Inheritance, Constructive Conscious Control, The Use of the Self, The Universal Constant of Living.*

It is a most curious fact that of the literally millions of educators who, for two generations, have so constantly appealed to Dewey's authority, only an infinitesimal handful has ever bothered to look into the method which Dewey himself regarded as absolutely fundamental to any effective system of education. The reason for this neglect is simple enough. Like everyone else, educators have a debauched kinesthetic sense; and, like everyone else, they do not know that their standards of physical right and wrong have been perverted. Long-standing habits of improper use lead them to believe that what they feel to be right and natural actually is right and natural. In fact, of course, it is wrong and unnatural, and feels right only because they are used to it. They cannot persuade themselves that anything is fundamentally wrong with their own psycho-physical instrument or with the psycho-physical instruments of their pupils. The disappointing results of education are attributed by them to various combinations of subsidiary and superficial causes, never to the fundamental cause of causes—improper use and loss of the natural standard of pyscho-physical health.

Most of us, as Alexander is never tired of insisting, are inveterate "end-gainers." We are so anxious to achieve some physical means whereby that end is to be gained. So far as we are concerned, any old means is good enough. But the nature of the universe is such that ends can never justify means. On the contrary, the means always determine the end. Thus the end proposed by the Allies in the First World War was "to make the world safe for democracy." But the means employed was unrestricted violence, and unrestricted violence is incapable of producing world-wide democracy. Unrestricted violence produces such things as fear, hatred and social chaos. Chaos is followed by dictatorship and dictatorship combined with general fear and hatred leads once more to unrestricted violence. This is an extreme case; but the principle it illustrates is universally valid. In the field of education, for example, a child is assigned a project. The end proposed is the learning of a set of facts and acquisition of certain skills and certain morally desirable attitudes. But among the means employed to achieve this end is the child's psycho-physical instrument. If (as is probably the case) this psycho-physical instrument has lost its standard of physical right and wrong and is a prey to bad habits, and if (as is virtually certain) nothing effective is being done to restore the standard and get rid of the bad habits, the ends proposed by well-meaning educators will not be achieved in their entirety. This failure to do anything effective about the psycho-physical instrument is surely one of the reasons why education has never justified the hopes of the idealists and reformers. Four generations ago James Mill expressed the belief that, if everybody could read and write, everything would be well forever. Personal liberty and democratic government would be assured, wars would cease, reason would everywhere prevail. Today everybody CAN read and write, and we find ourselves living in a world where war is incessant, liberty on the decline, democracy in peril, a world moreover where most of the beneficiaries of universal education read only the tabloids, the comics and murder mysteries.

Man, as we have seen, is a self associated with not-selves. By developing bad habits, the conscious ego and the personal subconscious interfere with the normal functioning of the deeper not-selves, from which we receive the animal grace of physical health and spiritual grace of insight. If we wish to educate the psycho-physical instrument, we must train people in the art of getting out of their own light. This truth has been discovered and rediscovered, again and again, by all the teachers of psycho-physical skills. In all the activities of life, from the most trivial to the most important, the secret of proficiency lies in an ability to combine two seemingly incompatible states—a state of maximum activity and a state of maximum relaxation. The fact that these incompatibles can actually coexist is due, of course, to the amphibious nature of the human being. That which must be relaxed is the ego and personal subconscious, that which must be active is the vegetative soul and the not-selves which lie beyond it. The physiological and spiritual not-selves with which we are associated cannot do their work effectively until the ego and personal subconscious learn to let go.

Descartes based the whole of his philosophy on the affirmation, *Cogito ergo sum*—I think, therefore I am. This sounds good, but unfortunately it doesn't happen to be true. The truth, as von Baader pointed out, is not *Cogito ergo sum* but *Cogitor ergo sum*. My existence does not depend on the fact that I am thinking; it depends on the fact that, whether I know it or not, I am being thought—being thought by a mind much greater than the consciousness which I ordinarily identify with myself. This fact is recognized by the tennis pro as it is recognized by the mystic, by the piano teacher as by the yogin, by the vocal coach as by the Zen master and the exponent of mental prayer. If I get out of my not-selves' light, I shall be illumined. If I stop anxiously *cogito-ing*, I shall give myself a chance of being *cogitor-ed* by a committee of indwelling intelligences that can deal with my problems a great deal better than I can. We must use our conscious will—but use it for the purpose of preventing our ego from succumbing to its old bad habits or in any other way eclipsing the inner lights. This does not mean, of course, that the conscious self can ever abdicate its position as knower, reasoner and maker of moral judgments. What it does mean is that we must give up the insane illusion that a conscious self, however virtuous and however intelligent, can do its work singlehanded and without assistance. Health is the harmony between self and not-selves, and proficiency in any field comes to those who have learned how to place the resources of their consciousness at the disposal of the unconscious. Genius is simultaneously inspiration and perspiration. It is no use inhaling unless we are prepared to sweat. And it is no use sweating unless we know how to inhale the life-giving airs that blow from worlds beyond our conscious selfhood.

The art of combining relaxation with activity has been invented and reinvented by the teachers of every kind of psycho-physical skill. Unfortunately these teachers have generally worked in isolation, each within the narrow field of his or her particular specialty. The activity for which they train their pupils is not the unregenerate activity for activity's sake, permitted and even encouraged by the Progressive Educationists. It is activity along the right lines, activity according to essentially sound principles. For this reason it will never do the harm which is done by unregenerate end-gaining. But though more or less harmless, it will be less beneficial than it would have been if it had been taught, not as an isolated special skill, but in conjunction with a general education of the kinesthetic sense, a total training in the use of the self, along the lines laid down by Alexander and so warmly recommended by John Dewey.

How much the indwelling not-selves can do for us, if we give them a chance, has been set forth in two remarkable little books, published within the last few years. The first is entitled *New Pathways to Piano Technique* by the late Luigi Bonpensiere. The second, *Zen and the Art of Archery*, has as its author a German psychologist, long resident in Japan, Dr. Eugen Herrigel. Each of these books bears witness to the same fundamental truth. When the conscious will is used to inhibit indulgence in the bad habits which have come to seem natural, when the ego has been taught to refrain from "straining every nerve," from desperately trying to "do something," when the personal subconscious has been induced to release its clutching tensions, the vegetative soul and the intelligences which lie beyond the vegetative soul can be relied upon to perform miracles.

As naturalists, we are familiar with the miracles performed by the indwelling intelligence of animals—miracles all the more remarkable because of the lack of intelligence displayed on the conscious level by the creatures concerned. I am not referring, of course, to the miracles of instinct; I am speaking of what may be called the *ad hoc* intelligence which animals sometimes display in situations never previously encountered in the evolutionary history of the species. For example, when a parrot uses its noise-making apparatus to imitate the articulate sounds produced by the radically dissimilar noise-making apparatus of a human being, some indwelling not-self is performing a miraculous feat of *ad hoc* intelligence. Or consider the extraordinary performance of the shearwater that was taken in a box from Wales to Venice (far beyond the normal range of the species), was released and turned up, in due course, at its original home. Something other, something far more intelligent than the conscious bird performed the miracle of imitation for the parrot, and the still more astounding miracle of homing for the shearwater. Our business as educators is to discover how human beings can make the best of both worlds—the world of self-conscious, verbalized intelligence and the world of the unconscious intelligences immanent in the mind-body, and always ready, if we give them half a chance, to do what, for the unaided ego, is the impossible.

JAMES D. KOERNER

James D. Koerner was born on February 3, 1923, in Cedar Rapids, Iowa. He attended public schools in the Midwest, and then went to Washington University in St. Louis, Missouri. He received his B.A. degree from Washington University in 1947, and his M.A. in 1949. In 1952 he received a Ph.D. in American Studies.

Koerner taught at Kansas State University from 1952 to 1954, and at the Massachusetts Institute of Technology from 1956 to 1958. From 1957 to 1959 he served as executive director of the Council for Basic Education, and was president of the Council from 1960 to 1967.

Koerner has conducted a number of educational studies, including a two-year study in England and Europe. He has contributed many articles to journals and newspapers including the *Atlantic Monthly, Harper's, The Saturday Review,* and *The Saturday Evening Post.* He is also the author of *The Case for Basic Education, Reform in Education,* and *The Miseducation of American Teachers.*

Primarily, Koerner desires a return to more basic subject matter in the schools, and has fought bitterly against education that is "Life Adjustment" or "Progressive." He believes that at the present time our education courses are too "watered down," and that they need to be upgraded or eliminated. Koerner has campaigned vigorously for more academic standards in our teacher-training institutions, as well as more basic subject matter in our schools from the earliest education one receives through the college level.

THE MISEDUCATION OF AMERICAN TEACHERS

James D. Koerner

American education produces no books that are what everybody says they should be—"objective." Education is as yet far too inexact a phenomenon for meticulous analysis. We are probably no closer now to basing education, that most tormented of subjects, on anything "objective" than mankind has ever been. Aristotle, whose glorious rage for order was occasionally frustrated, sounds reassuringly puzzled and modern as he surveys the education of his time and comments:

> It is clear then that there should be legislation about education and that it should be conducted on a public system. But consideration must be given to the question, what constitutes education and what is the proper way to be educated. At present there are differences of opinion as to the proper tasks to be set; for all peoples do not agree as to the things that the young ought to learn, either with a view to virtue or with a view to the best life, nor is it clear whether their studies should be regulated more with regard to intellect or with regard to character. And confusing questions arise out of the education that actually prevails, and it is not at all clear whether the pupils should practice pursuits that are practically useful, or morally edifying, or higher accomplishments—for all these views have the support of some judges...

Perhaps no creation of society as bound up as education is with the emotive ideals and desires of men can hope for any kind of precise discussion. Certainly not contemporary education, whose major characteristic is the imprecision of its peculiar language.

James D. Koerner. *The Miseducation of American Teachers*, Houghton Mifflin Company, Boston, Mass., 1963, pp. 1-10. © 1963 by James D. Koerner and reprinted by permission.

Despite the uncountable experiments that have been conducted in modern education, the tireless application of scientific method, the endless statistics, and all that which passes for research, educational programs in the United States continue to be constructed, and educational decisions continue to be made, on other than "objective" grounds; they continue to be chiefly acts of faith, hope, or charity. And educational books continue as always to be arguments based more on their authors' personal convictions than on any sort of recognized and accepted data.

This book, dealing with one of the most controversial and most protean areas in education, pretends to no scientific detachment, either in conception or execution. In conception, it grew out of what Albert Jay Nock once termed the first condition of progress, "a lively and peremptory dissatisfaction." Whether, in execution, this book also represents progress is something I can only hope for. My dissatisfaction arose initially, not by the way in which American teachers were educated, but by the way in which Americans were educated. I was led to my subject, that is, through an accumulation of unhappy impressions about the intellectual condition of American youth—before, in, and apart from, college. The signs and portents of miseducation in the United States are a tired though timeless topic: some people point to the low level of our public life and to the abdication of political responsibility by large numbers of citizens; some say the mass media and the persistence of mediocrity therein tell the truest story about American education; some point to the statistics on crime and juvenile delinquency and mental breakdown; some say they can't hire secretaries who can spell, punctuate, or file alphabetically, or workers who can read and comprehend directions or learn a new skill; and some point to the general irrationality and contempt for intellectualism so often evident in American life. The college instructor, for his part, is apt to point out that whatever else his incoming freshmen were doing before they arrived on campus, they were not mastering basic subjects. Nothing is clearer to him than the fact that his freshmen students, and others as well, have no useful grasp of a common body of elementary knowledge of Western culture or their own political or social institutions. They cannot be assumed to have a common acquaintance with any particular books or ideas and certainly not with the fundamentals of their own language. This unhappy condition necessitates the large and expensive remedial programs in basic subjects that most colleges operate; it also depresses standards in the regular classes.

The catalogue of complaint is long. How much justice it contains is the heart of the educational debate. Anyone who believes, as I do, that the complaints are just indeed is inevitably led to consider the education of teachers; for it is obvious that if their preparation is faulty changes must be made in the education of teachers before any substantive ones can be hoped for in public schools. After speculating with growing distress for over a decade about the enormous enterprise known as "teacher education" in our colleges and universities, I undertook a lengthy study of the subject. The study produced this book.

I would again emphasize that most arguments about teacher education no more lend themselves to "proof" than do debates about other educational problems. All the important questions one can ask about educating teachers must be answered on essentially suasive grounds; very few "data" exist on the best way to prepare people to teach in public schools or to administer them. Engineers are fond of referring to the degree of knowledge in technical fields at any given time as "the state of the art." In teacher education, the state of the art is infantile. An examination of the evidence available on the effectiveness of preparing teachers one way as against another leaves one in a familiar cul-de-sac, the only way out of which is through one's reasoned convictions. One can wholeheartedly agree with Mark Van Doren when he says,

> The education of teachers is an education in the liberal arts. When this education is good, and falls on the right ground, it produces persons with usable intellects and imaginations who know both what and why they are teaching. A teacher who can answer neither of those questions is no teacher, for thus he proves himself incapable of the one pleasure reserved for him among the pleasures possible to man: the pleasure of being intelligible.[1]

And one can agree with Sterling M. McMurrin, former United States Commissioner of Education, when he comments on how far short of this goal contemporary teacher education falls:

> The blunt fact is that many of our teachers are not properly qualified to handle the responsibility we have placed on them. This is our basic educational problem. Many of our teachers, for instance, lack native talent for teaching. It is a national scandal, moreover, that large numbers of them are inadequately prepared in the subject matter that they teach, as well as in the elements of

---

[1] *Liberal Education*, Beacon, 1959, pp. 175-76.

a genuinely liberal education. This is, in my view, the major weakness of American Education.[2]

But ultimately one recognizes such comments, as well as the opposing and contrasting ones that fill the educational air today, as statements of position, not subject to scientific verification.

The Miseducation of American Teachers is therefore filled with judgments, private evaluations, even prejudices if you like, as are, wittingly or not, all other books on the subject. Having said so much, I should also make clear that I have gone about studying teacher education as dispassionately as possible, have tried to proceed as undogmatically as I could, have freely modified many opinions with which I began, and have tried to base my assessments of the present state of the art on reasonable and demonstrable grounds. The book contains, in support of at least its main arguments, a considerable body of evidence gathered at first hand over an extended period of time. Whether the evidence is sufficient to justify the conclusions will depend on the reader's own convictions, for what I offer the reader are judgments based on much study and observation but based finally on conviction.

That being so, the reader has a right to ask after my educational principles and the point of view from which I examined the field of teacher education. These principles should not be construed as a "philosophy," a much-abused word in education. Although much is said throughout the field about the importance of one's "philosophy of education," and although training programs always have "courses" in this "subject," probably nobody active in teacher education today, with the doubtful exception of the Jesuits, has developed anything that could properly bear the name. And if had developed it he would no doubt, as George Santayana once remarked about academic philosophies, have little success in teaching it:

> That philosophers should be professors is an accident, and almost an anomaly. Free reflection about everything is a habit to be imitated, but not a subject to expound; and an original system, if the philosopher has one, is something dark, perilous, untested, and not ripe to be taught, nor is there much danger that any one will learn it.[3]

---

[2] *Ladies' Home Journal*, March, 1962, p. 6.
[3] *Character and Opinion in the United States*, Scribner, 1921, p. 35.

Even John Dewey, who was a considerable philosopher, could not be said to have formulated his diverse educational ideas around a "philosophy of education." He had his philosophy and he had his educational ideas, but there are few discernible bridges between, perhaps because, as he himself pointed out, philosophies have a kind of poetic and separatist life:

> The material out of which philosophy finally emerges is irrelevant to science and to explanation. It is figurative, symbolic of fears and hopes, made of imaginations and suggestions, not significant of a world of objective fact intellectually confronted. It is poetry and drama, rather than science, and apart from scientific truth and falsity, rationality or absurdity of fact in the same way that poetry is independent of these things.[4]

Yet it is also true that one's educational ideas must presuppose SOME view of man, however undeveloped or unspoken, some view of the nature of reality and of cognition; for education "is obliged from the outset," to use Jacques Maritain's words "to answer the question, 'What is man?' which the philosophical sphinx is asking." Unfortunately, modern education does not meet this obligation, does not answer the question, does not even ask it. Most educators, in forming their views and certainly in carrying out instructional programs, operate on a less elevated plane. Nevertheless, the programs they do create are implicit evidence of their view of man's purpose and his potential.

I intrude at this point my own educational views, which I cannot dignify as either a philosophy or a theory of education, only because these views may throw some light for any interested reader on the mind-set with which I approached the field of teacher education. Presumably anyone attempting to evaluate the preparation of teachers must do so from some fundamental point of view about educational purpose, else he would have no basis upon which to make judgments. My point of view is this: Whatever our attitude toward the ultimate questions that have always confronted mankind, whether we believe man to be a divinely inspired creature or merely a cosmic accident, we have no choice but to assume that Western civilization is good, at least more good than bad; and that whatever hopes we have for the future will have to be realized through the continuation and improvement of that civilization,

---

[4] *Reconstruction in Philosophy*, Beacon, 1948, p. 7.

building on all that has gone before. Our civilization is the product of a long and painful process of taming, training, and refining the human animal, a process made possible by two characteristics that distinguish man from all other creatures: intelligence and compassion.

These virtues have been the means by which man has raised himself from savagery—his intelligence, by which he has disciplined himself and enabled himself to investigate and in some measure understand and control both himself and his environment; his compassion, by which he has muted his natural selfishness and his continuing capacity for barbarism, and by which he has brought dignity and nobility into his own affairs. If it is true that, as Santayana has suggested, "Perhaps the only true dignity of man is his capacity to despise himself," it is true only because of man's unique capacity to see how far short he still falls of what the ancients called the SUMMUM BONUM—how wide the gulf still is between his achievements and his possibilities, between what is and what might be. The job of education, I believe, is to try to bridge this gulf.

Education can best do this job by training the intellect of each new generation vigorously and systematically in those subjects that are the most fruitful for man's continuing development. At the same time education must seek to awaken the individual's moral faculty and to discipline his will. It follows, then, that young people have far more to unite them educationally than to divide them. They have their humanity itself, their country, and the cultural and intellectual heritage wrought for them, through infinite travail, by those who preceded them. Not merely for the protection and advancement of society, but especially for the individual's own sake, young people desperately need to acquaint themselves with that heritage, with what Matthew Arnold called "the best that has been thought and said in the world"; they need to come to close quarters with great men and great achievements and to sense something of the agony and the joy experienced by those who have moved the world forward.

For most young people these ends are best attained through an education based, not on the development of what, symptomatically, have come to be called "marketable skills" or on vocational training or on ways of adjusting to society, but on the principal areas of human knowledge: ENGLISH AND FOREIGN LANGUAGES, HISTORY, MATHEMATICS, AND THE NATURAL SCIENCES. These subjects are not arbitrary divisions of knowledge, as they are so often alleged to be by educationists,[5] but are the divisions, each with its own techniques of research and advancement, that men over long periods have found to produce the most fruitful results. They are the subjects that create other secondary subjects useful in higher education and often important fields in their own right, but which at the public school level are inappropriate. In the common schools of a free society, the question of priorities should be compelling, for there is time only for the essential, generative subjects, which best serve the needs of all men, as citizens and human beings. If our public schools could insure a minimum literacy in these basic areas for most students, while pushing students with the requisite capacity to greater depths, one could hardly ask for more. But this much assumes a view of man's potential that educationists and many others are loath to grant. It assumes that most children are capable of being educated to a significant degree—at different rates, to be sure—in the basic subjects. There is no body of evidence acceptable to most educationists to support this assumption, and it may well be ill-founded; on the other hand, there is no cogent evidence to support opposing or contrasting views. Until we know immeasurably more than we now know about the mind and heart of man, one's argument for a public education grounded in a few fundamental subjects must remain essentially hortatory.

HOW this kind of basic education can best be carried on in a classroom is another question. Let us by all means adopt those methods of progressivism that involve the student as actively as possible in the learning process. And let us by all means champion those views, whether coming from a Montaigne, a Rousseau, or a Dewey, that seek to reduce the cruelties or the senseless coercions of the classroom that, it is said, used to constitute education. Let us agree with Dewey when he decries, as he does in a thousand places, the meaningless rigidities of American schools:

---

[5] An opprobrious term to many persons who prefer to call themselves "professional educators"; i.e., educational administrators, professors of education, and others whose careers are in the field of education as such. However, I use the term with no unfavorable connotations attached, but merely as a better means of identification than "professional educator," a term which, after all, ought to encompass the liberal arts professor and others whose careers are in education. I take my cue not only from traditional usage (Horace Mann, for example, uses the term many times), but from many contemporary educationists, such as Theodore Brameld, who feels that "the word is a perfectly good one to distinguish those engaged in the practice of teaching teachers."—*Education for the Emerging Nation*, Harper, 1961, p. 195.

> When we think of the docility of the young we first think of the stores of information adults wish to impose and the way of acting they want to reproduce. Then we think of the insolent coercions, the insinuating briberies, the pedagogic solemnities by which the freshness of youth can be faded and its vivid curiosities dulled. Education becomes the art of taking advantage of the helplessness of the young; the forming of habits becomes a guarantee for the maintenance of hedges of custom.[6]

Let us do everything we can to facilitate the learning process, but let the "learning" remain in it. Let us not confuse, as so much of progressivism did, the pleasant with the important, the temporary with the permanent, or "the broad primrose path" which, in Whitehead's words, "leads to a nasty place," with the long and rocky road to genuine education.

It may be that most men are not, after all, capable of such education. It may be that the view of man propounded most eloquently by Albert Jay Nock, and echoed unwittingly by modern educationists, is nearer the truth. It was his conviction that only a tiny minority of men was capable of serious education and that our greatest mistake, from which arose all our insoluble educational problems, was in our failure to heed this fact and in our fruitless attempts to educate everybody. The result, as he saw it, was chaos in which those few persons capable of being educated and serving both themselves and their culture were wasted while the many were exposed to a mishmash of courses in subjects that could not possibly interest them or mean anything to them. Let the majority of citizens be given vocational training so that they can become useful and productive citizens, but let us not squander our resources, said Nock, on futile attempts at anything so absurd as universal education. Surveying our education history, he found,

> ... three most serious errors in the theory upon which the mechanics of our educational system were designed. This theory contemplates a fantastic and impracticable idea of equality, a fantastic and impracticable idea of democracy, and a fantastically exaggerated idea of the importance of literacy in assuring the support of a sound and enlightened public order. It is not necessary, I think, to go further in the examination of our educational theory, after finding in it three errors of the first magnitude.[7]

---

[6] *Human Nature and Conduct*, Henry Holt, 1922, p. 64.
[7] *The Theory of Education in the United States*, Harcourt, 1932, p. 44.

Nock, I believe, was wrong. But I can only appeal likewise to our collective experience, and perhaps to faith as well, to support the idea that the great majority of people can respond well to liberal education when it is conducted well. Universal "education," although we have never given it a trial, and not universal "marketable skills," is a wholly realistic expectation for the United States. But we can go only as far in that direction as the quality of our teachers permits.

JACQUES MARITAIN

Jacques Maritain was born in Paris, France, on November 18, 1882. He received his early education at the Lycée Henri IV, and later attended the Sorbonne, at which time he also attended the lectures of Henri Bergson at the College de France. After receiving his Ph.D. both Maritain and his wife Raissa were converted to Roman Catholicism in 1906, after which he undertook an extensive study of the philosophy of Saint Thomas Aquinas, particularly in its relationship to the modern world.

In 1913 Maritain became professor of modern history and philosophy at the Institut Catholique, which was founded to offset the skeptical tendencies of the Sorbonne. He also taught at College Stanislas in Paris, the Petit Seminare in Versailles, as well as Columbia University and Princeton University in the United States.

During World War II Maritain assisted the deGaulle movement, and in 1945 was appointed French Ambassador to the Vatican. After spending three years in Rome he returned to Princeton University in 1948 where he remained until 1953.

Maritain has written a number of books on religion, philosophy, and education, including *Education at the Crossroads, Education of Man, Freedom and the Modern World, The Range of Reason,* and *True Humanism.*

Primarily, the writings of Maritain have been considered as a technical exposition of Scholastic philosophy with regard to politics, art, education, and religion. Maritain believes that education should convey some sense of the spiritual heritage of civilization; and the confusion of modern life, he points out, is caused by the fact that people know nothing about the soul as well as our moral and religious tradition.

Maritain feels that modern Progressivism has been turned into a "babysitting" operation where children receive little challenge or discipline. In addition to "learning by doing" Maritain feels that there must be some recognition in education of the fact that real education begins with insights and intuitions based on *a priori* principles.

EDUCATION AT THE CROSSROADS

Jacques Maritain

We come now to the special tasks which the present crisis of civilization and the conditions of the postwar world are to impose upon education. These tasks are manifold and momentous. As a result of the present disintegration of family life, of a crisis in morality and the break between religion and life, and finally of a crisis in the political state and the civic conscience, and the necessity for democratic states to rebuild themselves according to new patterns, there is a tendency, everywhere, to burden education with remedying all these deficiencies. This involves a risk of warping educational work, especially when immediate transformations are expected from its supposedly magic power. Yet extraneous burdens superadded to the normal task of education must be accepted for the sake of the general welfare.

In such a situation, the duty of educators is obviously twofold: they have both to maintain the essentials of humanistic education and to adapt them to the present requirements of the common good.

Education has its own essence and its own aims. This essence and these essential aims, which deal with the formation of man and the inner liberation of the human person, must be preserved, whatever the superimposed burdens may be. It is not a question of refusing the latter. But if they were taken up in the wrong way, so as to warp the essential human values of education; or if the school, conceived according to some totalitarian pattern as an organ of the political state, were to replace the free and normal agencies provided by nature and by God for the upbringing of man, then the common good, for the sake of

Jacques Maritain. *Education at the Crossroads,* Yale University Press, New Haven, Conn., 1943, pp. 91-93, 94-103. © 1943 by Yale University Press and reprinted by permission.

which the superadded burdens must be assumed, would be not ensured, but betrayed. The remedy would only have aggravated the evil.

It is to be expected that in the world of tomorrow the educational system will take on ever-growing importance and amplitude, and become, still more than today, the basic and crucial function of a civil community aware of the dignity of the people, and of the destined rise of the common man. Since we have here a matter of public interest, the state cannot hold itself aloof from it, and its help as well as its supervision will be accordingly required. Many changes in the present status of colleges and universities will probably take place. The number of educational institutions founded and supported by the state will probably increase. All this is a normal process in itself. But it must be brought about in freedom and for freedom, and the relationship between state and school must be rightly understood.

Here we face again the importance of the pluralist principle, which grants to the manifold groups arising from free association the greatest possible autonomy, and bases the state's superior authority on the recognition of the rights of these groups. As concerns the educational system, the pluralist principle implies basically academic freedom. Not only does it stress the right to found schools, which is open to everyone qualified and complying with the laws of the state. It also demands that diverse teaching institutions be free to join with each other in several unions or organizations which would be prevented by law from encroaching upon the basic liberties of their members, but could establish general regulations valid inside each union. It is by the agreements concluded between the state and some general board composed of the representatives of these unions (including the unions of schools and colleges supported by the state) that any justifiable intervention of the state in educational matters might take place.

An important role should be granted to the parents' associations, which would make their desires heard by the educational body and whose claims could counterbalance the demands of the state. The role of labor unions and other great economic or cultural organizations, which might possibly become the founders and trustees of a number of privately endowed teaching institutions, should also be taken into consideration.

If we consider more closely the added tasks which I have mentioned, the first has to do with the present crisis in morality. The task of moral re-education is really a matter of public emergency. Every serious observer recognizes the fact that children have not only to be trained in proper conduct, law observance, and politeness, but that this very training remains deficient and precarious if there is no genuine internal formation. That the teachers in public schools may not face unruliness and violence, moral authority must be recognized; and there must be a serious teaching of moral principles, I mean as grounded on truth rather than as suitable to social convenience. This surely involves more than the theory that children should first set free the instincts of primitive man in order to purge themselves of them.

* * *

Yet what our present problem asks us to take into consideration is the large number of parents who are opposed to any religious education for their children. Here we are confronted anew with a peculiar task required today from the school system, and which is momentous. Additional emphasis should be brought to the teaching of natural morality. The normal way of giving this teaching, which is to have it embodied in the humanities, literature, and history ... does not suffice in the face of the tremendous degradation of ethical reason which is observable today. For the moment the evil seems more apparent in our ideas than in our conduct, I mean in still civilized countries. Exhausted and bewildered by dint of false and dehumanized philosophy, reason confesses its impotence to justify any ethical standards. To such a disease of human intelligence and conscience, special remedies should be given, not only through the badly needed revival of religious faith but also through a revival of the moral power of reason. Accordingly, if teachers may be found whose reason is healthier than that of their students, special teaching should be provided, in schools and colleges, for the principles of natural morality.

Let us observe at this point that the field in which natural morality feels most at home, and least deficient, is the field of our temporal activities, or of political, civic, and social morality: because the virtues proper to this field are essentially natural ones, directed toward the good of civilization; whereas in the field of personal morality, the whole scope of the moral life cannot be comprehended by reason with regard to our real system of conduct in actual existence, without taking into account the supratemporal destiny of man. So the teaching of natural morality will naturally tend to lay stress on what may be called the ethics of political life and of civilization. Which is all to the good (for here it enjoys its maximum strength and practical truth) provided that it resist the temptation of neglecting or disparaging personal morality, which is the root of all morality. Above all it should resist the temptation of warping and perverting all its work by making itself a tool of the state to shape youth according to the collective pattern supposedly needed by the pride, greed, or myths of the earthly community.

Now, since we are dealing with morality and moral teaching, we must not overlook the practical truth which is of the greatest moment in this regard: as to the actual uprightness of the will and human conduct, knowledge and sound teaching are necessary but are surely not enough. In order for us rightly to judge what to do in a particular case, our reason itself depends on the uprightness of our will, and on the decisive movement of our very freedom. The melancholy saying of Aristotle, contrasting with the Socratic doctrine that virtue is only knowledge, is to be recalled in this connection: "To know," he said, "does little, or even nothing, for virtue."[1]

What does a great deal for virtue is love: because the basic hindrance to moral life is egoism, and the chief yearning of moral life liberation from oneself; and only love, being the gift of oneself, is able to remove this hindrance and to bring this yearning to fulfillment. But love itself is surrounded by our central egoism, and in perpetual danger of becoming entangled in and recaptured by it, whether this egoism makes the ones we love a prey to our devouring self-love or merges them in the ruthless self-love of the group, so as to exclude all other men from our love. Love does not regard ideas or abstractions or possibilities, love regards existing persons. God is the only person whom human love can fly to and settle in, so as to embrace also all other persons and be freed from egotistic self-love.

Love, human love as well as divine love, is not a matter of training or learning, for it is a gift; the love of God is a gift of nature and of grace: that is why it can be the first precept. How could we be commanded to put into action a power which we have not received or may not first receive? There are no human methods or techniques of getting or developing charity, any more than any other kind of love. There is, never-

---

[1] II *Ethic.*; cf. Saint Thomas Aquinas, III *Sent.*, dist. 33, 9, 2.

theless, education in this matter: an education which is provided by trial and suffering, as well as by the human help and instruction of those whose moral authority is recognized by our conscience.

Here the educational sphere involved is first of all the family. Is not family love the primary pattern of any love uniting a community of men? Is not fraternal love the very name of that neighborly love which is but one with the love of God? No matter what deficiencies the family group may present in certain particular cases, no matter what trouble and disintegration the economic and social conditions of our day have brought to family life, the nature of things cannot be changed. And it is in the nature of things that the vitality and virtues of love develop first in the family. Not only the examples of the parents, and the rules of conduct which they inculcate, and the religious habits and inspiration which they further, and the memories of their own lineage which they convey, in short the educational work which they directly perform, but also, in a more general way, the common experiences and common trials, endeavors, sufferings and hopes, and the daily labor of family life, and the daily love which grows up in the midst of cuffs and kisses, constitute the normal fabric where the feelings and the will of the child are naturally shaped. The society made up by his parents, his brothers and sisters, is the primary human society and human environment in which, consciously and subconsciously, he becomes acquainted with love and from which he receives his ethical nourishment. Here both conflicts and harmonies have educational value; a boy who has experienced common life with his sisters, a girl who has done so with her brothers, have gained unawares invaluable and irreplaceable moral advance as regards the relationship between the sexes. Over and above all, family love and brotherly love create in the heart of the child that hidden recess of tenderness and repose the memory of which man so badly needs, and in which, perhaps after years of bitterness, he will immerse himself anew each time a natural trend to goodness and peace awakens in him.

The second burden superadded to the normal task of education deals with the needs of the state and the political commonwealth in the postwar period. In this connection Professor Clarke, whom I have already quoted[2] warns us that "it is not for this generation to know the settled peace and quiet effectiveness of an assured and straight-moving

_____
[2] F. Clarke, *A Review of Educational Thought*, London, 1942.

education." He observes that the sense of amplitude and freedom enjoyed in so high a degree by his country's traditional education implied in reality the common acceptance, by the entire social environment, of strong and imperative mental and political patterns, of customs, habits, and standards deeply, subconsciously rooted. Thus the freest educational system involves in reality an authoritative character, "least obvious," he goes on to say, "just when it is most complete and unquestioned; when it is so secure, so absolute, so all-pervading that it feels no need to be obtrusive."

It is clear that for the educational body as well as for the individual citizen, freedom, rights, and autonomy have responsibility, duties, and moral obligations as their correlatives. In a human commonwealth, freedom and authority are as necessary for one another, by virtue of the nature of things, as their occasional conflicts are inevitable in actual fact. Political authority, that right to direct and to be obeyed for the sake of the general welfare, is not opposed to human freedom, but required by it. In contradistinction to despotic authority, which directs a man toward the private and individual good of his master, and which places the one directed in a state of servitude, political authority directs free men toward the good, not of the one who directs, but of the multitude as a whole, or of the body politic—a common good which is desired by each component of the body politic, insofar as he is a part of it, and which is to flow back upon each one. Political authority, which is naught without justice, requires by its very nature free obedience based on conscience and moral obligation. The power of compulsion is only an additional property, arising from the fact that this command of justice may be, and is often in fact, disregarded by some. But without genuine authority, that is, without the very right to be obeyed by virtue of man's moral conscience, this power of compulsion is but tyrannical.

These basic principles apply to groups and particular bodies as well as to the individuals in civil society. The educational body, to the very extent that it is free and autonomous, is bound in conscience to the common good. To the very extent that it is entrusted with an all-important function in the common good, it is bound in conscience to feel responsible toward the entire community, and to take into consideration the requirements of the general welfare. Political authority, in the broad sense in which I use the word, has not only to protect the freedom of teaching but also to guide it toward the good of the whole, as far as a matter essential to the very life of the whole is involved.

Indeed, the time of anarchical freedom, which is but a false freedom, is gone. The crucial point is to pass on to an age, not of servitude, but of real and organic freedom. As concerns education, this is not the moment to accept any philosophy which would warp its true essence, but rather to affirm and maintain this essence more than ever. I am afraid the new insistence on authority, therefore, if it departs from the unchangeable lines of the education of man, may perhaps deviate toward rather despotical educational philosophies.

Professor Clarke's definition of education, as the "self-perpetuation of an accepted culture, . . . of a culture which is the life of a determinate society," is only given in terms of social qualities, and is not adequate. If an accepted culture is permeated with errors, cruelties, or slavery, the task of education is not to perpetuate it, but to strive to change it. No doubt Professor Clarke would not deny that; and when he approves of the statement by Professor Hocking, "Education must produce the type," he approves too of the second part of the same statement, "and it must provide for growth beyond the type."[3]

Yet this very formula, even with its additional correction, remains terribly biological and sociological. Doubtless because education is immersed in a given culture and conveys it to youth, it produces in actual fact an average cultural type—but without having chosen such a task as its aim. Its real aim is to make a man. If the type is wrong, to grow beyond the type will perhaps result in something still worse. Education should essentially aim not at producing the type but at liberating the human person.

The educational philosophy of the production of the type is naturally akin to the trend of thought of Plato's *Laws*; for Plato the type must be produced by virtue of a "music" which is imposed upon education by the state. Modern states, especially modern states in the making, with their dependence on the masses and public opinion, and their crucial need of creating unity and unanimity in an emergency, will look upon such philosophy with special complacency. And they will take the application of this philosophy upon themselves. Then it would be no longer a question of Plato or of his *Laws*. The state would summon education to make up for all that is lacking in the surrounding order in the matter of common political inspiration, stable customs and traditions, common inherited standards, moral unity and unanimity; it would urge education

---

[3] W. E. Hocking, *Man and the State*, Yale University Press, New Haven, 1926.

to perform an immediate political task and, in order to compensate for all the deficiencies in civil society, to turn out in a hurry the "type" fitted to the immediate needs of the political power. Accordingly education would become a function directly and uniquely dependent on the management of the state, and the educational body an organ of state machinery. As a result of the extraneous and unnatural burden thus imposed upon education, and of the subsequent annexation of the educational task by the state, both the essence and freedom of education would be ruined. Such a process can succeed only with that utter perversion of the political state which is the totalitarian state, conceiving of itself as free from justice and as the supreme rule of good and evil. With a democratic state, this educational method would only lead to perfect disappointment. If the impact of the state upon education were conceived in this way, we should have to defend education against the state. In this connection it is not reassuring to read in the last book by so valuable and freedom-loving an educator as Dr. Meiklejohn the following statements: "Education is an expression of the will of some social 'organism, instinct with one life, moved by one mind.' Teacher and pupil ... are both agents of the state."[4]

Yet the situation described by Professor Clarke remains undeniable. In normal circumstances, as he rightly points out, especially with strong aristocratic and traditional structures like those of England, the body politic regulates education less by way of the state than through the spontaneous influence of a stable and all-pervading social and cultural order. When this spontaneous regulation is lacking, the political body's regulation has inevitably to take place through state supervision. Such a supervision, nevertheless, should never imply any illegitimate interference of the state with the means and intrinsic norms of teaching. It should be strictly limited to those matters which directly interest the public welfare: the state might keep the educational body informed of society's needs for certain categories of activities and for the training concerned; above and over all, the state should see to it that no trend whatever opposed to the values which have been agreed upon as the very basis of common life and common fellowship may ever develop in education, and that the values in question should be carefully elucidated and firmly insisted upon.

Moreover peace, if peace is actually won, will be not a static but a

---

[4] Alexander Meiklejohn, *Education Between Two Worlds,* Harper & Row, New York, 1942, p. 279.

dynamic and militant peace, which will require a tremendous effort of moral, social, and political reconstruction as well as of defense against the remainders of those egotistic and anarchical trends and that greed for domination which poison the world today. The freedom enjoyed by education, therefore, will not be a quiet and easygoing, peacefully expanding freedom, but a tense and fighting one. Yet while changing its mood and taking on a new and more stringent style, it can and must remain freedom. We may be sure that the educational system will not need any obtrusive pressure of the state in order to help the effort of the body politic toward moral unity. It will spontaneously cooperate, by sharing in the common inspiration. Democracies are aware today of their long carelessness in failing to defend and stress their own principles, their own intellectual and moral roots, in their own schools. They do not need to borrow totalitarian methods in order to remedy this lack. The great thing is that the democratic state itself have its own philosophy of life and society, and have faith in it. The generality of educators will be carried along on this faith, by virtue of good will or of conformity. Unity cannot be imposed by force and from without. Unity is but a result, as is peace, a result of actual inner inspiration, good will, and love for a common ideal clearly affirmed and a common task to be performed.

All of the new conditions I have mentioned may be satisfied without altering the essence of education. At any rate this very essence must remain intact. For the sake of the new civilization we are fighting for, it is more than ever necessary that education be the education of man, and education for freedom, the formation of free men for a free commonwealth. It is in education that freedom has its deepest human recess, where the reserves of freedom are kept alive.

The present war creates an immense need for technology and technical training. This need must obviously be satisfied, because of public emergency, while we maintain as far as possible the root exigencies of education. But after the war, however great the need for technicians may be, it would be an irremediable mistake not to return to the primacy and integrity of liberal education. Supposing that the training in liberal arts may be completed at nineteen, according to our ideal curriculum, enough time would remain thereafter for any intensive technical training, and this training itself should keep pace with that free and disinterested cultivation of the spirit which I emphasized apropos of the university period. For here we are confronted with the primary conditions of a community of free men.

ASHLEY MONTAGU

Ashley Montagu was born in London, England, on June 28, 1905. He attended University College, the University of London, from 1922 to 1925 where he studied physical anthropology and biology. He also attended Columbia University and then went to the University of Florence where he worked with the Institute of Royal Academy of Ethnology and Anthropology. In 1929 he assumed the position of curator of physical anthropology at Medical Museum in London, England. He received his Ph.D. in anthropology from Columbia University in 1937, and has taught at New York University, Hahnemann Medical College and Hospital in Philadelphia, and at Rutgers University.

Montagu has achieved a great deal of popularity through his writings in magazines and newspapers as well as his frequent appearances on TV. He has written a number of books dealing with anthropology and education including On Being Human, The Natural Superiority of Women, The Direction of Human Development, The American Way of Life, and Education and Human Relations.

Montagu feels that teachers in America instruct rather than educate, that they build-in knowledge rather than cause it to grow. He feels that the three R's have their place but that a fourth R should be added, i.e., Relation, so that students could be taught to relate themselves warmly, cooperatively, and creatively to other human beings. For a person to be educated, he feels that the person must first be humanized, and he cannot do this without learning how to love other human beings. A study of anthropology, he believes, helps to develop the kind of humanizing he means, and helps to create individuals who would pass these traits on to their children.

EDUCATION AND HUMAN RELATIONS

Ashley Montagu

The teachers of the young are at once the most important and the most privileged of all those agencies which enter into the functioning of society. Theirs is the most fundamental of all creative social functions; for what can exceed in social importance the task of molding the mind and helping to form the character of the growing member of society? The adult is, to a very large extent, what his teachers have made him, and in this very real sense, the true, unacknowledged legislators of any land are its teachers. There are many among us who owe whatever humanity they may have arrived at, and whatever claim they may have to the ability of using their minds critically, to the influence of a few childhood teachers; and I am afraid that there are those among us, too, who have suffered more pain and misery under the inflexible minds of too many unsympathetic teachers than they would perhaps care to recall. But it is as necessary to recall such unfortunate experiences as it is to recollect those happier ones which have meant so much to us, for there can hardly be a more immediate method by which to prove to ourselves the superlative value and importance of the sympathetic teacher.

In our democracy the purposes and methods of education have perhaps received more critically intelligent and experimental consideration than has been the case in any other country in the world, and as one important consequence of this it is now coming to be generally recognized that the educative process consists of much more than merely drawing out what is within each individual and filling him up with a lot of heterogeneous information. Reading, writing, and arithmetic are im-

Ashley Montagu. *Education and Human Relations*, Grove Press, Inc., New York, 1958, pp. 11-23. © 1958 by Ashley Montagu and reprinted by permission.

portant—but not indispensable. A competence in such subjects by no means equips the individual to lead the life of an adequate human being or confers upon him the ability to be socially sympathetic to, and individually interested in, other human beings, of whatever country, caste, or color they may be. Indeed, a strong case might be made out for the claim that the three R's make it possible for an individual to be less of a human being with them than he would have been without them.

Indeed, what do the mass of people do with their ability to read and write and add up a column of figures? What, presumably, they have socially learned to do. They buy their morning newspapers as an addict buys his opium, there to read the day's calendar of murders, rapes, lynchings, fires, kidnapings, political chicanery, municipal holdups, and so on. Is it not a sufficient commentary upon the educational system of our schools when we reflect that tens of millions of individuals, of their own free will, every day purchase and read the kind of papers that they do? Who can observe mature individuals enchanted by the fantastic puerilities of the "funnies" without being convinced that somewhere something is somehow wrong? The ability of such individuals to write is used for all sorts of purposes, perhaps the strangest being to prove their literacy at a voting booth. While their ability to add up a column of figures they would seem to use chiefly for the purpose of scoring up the number of runs or touchdowns made during the season by their particular heroes.

This is, of course, a very one-sided and somewhat exaggerated picture, but does it not touch off something of the essential truth? The truth that education is for us, as human beings, valueless unless it is informed by the principle of humanity? For what is the use of any education unless it renders the individual capable of thinking, feeling, and knowing that nothing which is human is alien to him? Can we ask for a more tragic exhibition of antihuman behavior than we are at present witnessing, when members of the same society turn against one another for no offense greater than the fortuitous association of an individual with a particular religion or a difference in skin color? Such behavior usually goes by the names of religious or race prejudice or religious or racial intolerance. We have already seen, and some of us have experienced, the extremes to which such prejudices may be made to go in Europe. Can such things happen here? Certainly—but it must be our task, as teachers of human beings, to see that they do not. As teachers we can do a great deal toward making humanity safe for the world. Perhaps we cannot do everything, but we can do the most essential part of the spadework.

Right here and now we can introduce into our schools the long overdue teaching of the facts concerning race. These are simple and clear enough, and there is nothing in the least recondite or mysterious about them. It is through the lower- and upper-grade schools that the most significant work can be done in clarifying the minds of individuals concerning the facts of race, and in educating them in the proper attitudes of mind toward that subject. Let us teach geography, but instead of presenting facts of geography in the customary manner, let us humanize its teaching and furnish its field with the living peoples who inhabit this earth. Let us teach our pupils and students what we know concerning the peoples of the earth, and make clear their respective value for one another and their potentialities for civilization as a whole. Relations between other human beings and ourselves form the most important of all the experiences and situations of our lives. Would it not be incredible, did we not know it for a fact, that in our society human beings are permitted to enter into such relations without being equipped with the most elementary understanding of the nature of such relations? Certainly little or no attempt is made to supply them with the facts relating to race as made available by science; but we do, on the other hand, supply them with the kind of information which provides fertile ground for the development of race prejudices.[1] Here then, is a most important field in which a great and valuable pioneer work demands to be done.[2]

But let no one be deceived into believing that, by teaching the simple facts of race, the problems of race will thus be automatically solved. Tolerance of other human groups, like all tolerance, is a matter of simple human decency; and decency is an attitude of mind which is, for the most part, culturally produced. Whether races or ethnic groups are biologically equal or not is an utterly irrelevant consideration where tolerance as an attitude of mind is concerned. Where differences exist between peoples it is surely obvious that tolerance ought to increase in proportion to the magnitude of the differences which are believed to exist between ourselves and others. The truly humane mind not only insists

---

[1] See E. V. Baker, *The Historical Outlook*, February, 1933.
[2] For a tentative program, most interestingly set out, see *The Teaching Biologist*, vol. 9, 1939, pp. 17-47; also M. F. Ashley Montagu, *Man's Most Dangerous Myth: The Fallacy of Race*, Harper, New York, 1952.

upon the right of everyone to be different, but rejoices in most of those differences and is not indifferent to those which it may dislike. Difference and variety in human beings are the salt of life and the basis of collective achievement. Until this is realized and such an attitude of mind becomes part of the heritage of every individual, no amount of instruction in the biological facts concerning "race" will ever succeed in eliminating race prejudices. Race prejudice can ultimately be regarded as merely the effect of a poorly or incompletely developed personality. If race prejudice is ever to be eliminated from our society, then, society must assume the task of educating the individual, not so much in the facts about "race" as in the processes which lead to the development of a completely integrated human being. The solution here, as in so much else, lies in education. Education for humanity first and above all else, and in the facts afterwards. For what is the use of facts unless they are humanely understood and intelligently used?

Here lies the great opportunity for those unacknowledged legislators of the world, the teachers of our young.

In our schools we teach the three R's; the fourth R, relations, human relations, it has been said, we do not teach. I think this is no more true than to say that what is wrong with most Americans today is that they have no values. Unfortunately, the trouble with most Americans is not that they have no values, but that they have too many values of the wrong kind. Similarly, it is not true to say that we fail to teach human relations in our schools. We do teach such relations not only in a negative way, but we teach them in an unmistakably positive way. And it is, on the whole, a way which is of the most unfortunate kind.

In our schools organized instruction in human relations, when it is not left to the coach on the football or baseball team, is generally more honored in the breach than in the observance. But unorganized instruction in human relations occurs in all schools. From the principal to the janitor, children learn how to behave in relations to others. Not so much from what they say, as from what they do. Example is stronger than precept, and imitation is the most immediate form of learning. Words have no meaning other than the action they produce. And in our schools words are activated by what the teachers believe. From every standpoint, then, it is important that teachers, the unacknowledged legislators of the world, shall believe in the right things. For unless they do so, their words and conduct, no matter how noble the sentiments they are supposed to express, will be recognized for the counterfeit coin that they are. There are today thousands of teachers in our schools who are teaching race prejudice to their pupils. They do this not by means of prepared courses in the subject, but by their attitudes on any matter in which human relations arise, by a look, an expression, an inflection of the voice, or the weighting of a word. Though they have never been formulated in so many words, the views of such teachers on the subject of race and race relations are clearly understood by, and exert a considerable influence upon, their pupils. Such teachers do not belong in a school. The principal function of the teacher is, or should be, to help prepare the child for living a humane and co-operative life, not to infect his mind with the antihuman virus of racism.

No one should ever be permitted to become a teacher of the young unless by temperament, attitudes, and training he is fitted to do so. The teacher is the most important of all the public servants of the community; for what service can be more important to the community than the molding of the mind and conditioning of the social behavior of the future citizen? The anything but princely stipends with which he is rewarded for his services suggests that our society does not recognize the true value or function of the teacher.

The school, in America, is a place of instruction. It is not really a place of education in the proper sense of that word. In conformity with the requirements of a burgeoning industrial civilization, techniques and technology are at a premium. What can be used to succeed in such a society becomes that which is most emphasized during the learning period; the rest is sheer luxury, "frills," "school-larnin'," "academic stuff," or simply "points." From such a standpoint it is but natural that Americans should come to believe that the function of the school is essentially to teach the three R's in terms of the crude needs of an industrial civilization.

Clearly, values here are sadly mixed. They are the values of the world's largest industrial civilization. The value "success" in such a civilization is measured in terms of dollars. A man's worth in such a civilization is not his quality but his quantity, quantity of dollars, possessions.

Validation of success in terms of externals has become the mark of our civilization. In such a value system, human relations take on the ethical values of the salesman. To succeed you must know how to win friends and influence people, you must be "a good mixer," you must have lots of "contacts," and you must be able to "sell" people. The idols of the market place reign supreme. Competition is the most powerful law of the land. The competitive personality governed by the ideals of an industrial society must always be out in front. He must be better than others, for to be so yields the greatest returns. In the world of a person so conditioned it is taken for granted that some persons are inferior to others in their capacity to achieve. To most such persons the notion that there are whole groups of mankind which are unimprovably inferior is not only acceptable but indispensably necessary, for it constitutes at once a proof of the validity of the system and an incentive to go ahead and reap its benefits. It is a fully fledged belief in the doctrine of the survival of the fittest. The fit are those who are going to succeed or who have already succeeded, while the unfit are those who are not going to succeed, and it is, of course, most convenient and useful to know beforehand who is, and what groups of men are *not*, going to succeed.

It will readily be seen that the doctrine of racism is admirably adapted to the practices of imperialism and to the requirements of a ruggedly individualistic competitive society, "a graduated democracy," as one sociologist cynically put it. Not that such doctrines are indispensable correlates of such political and social practices; they do, however, provide the most convenient rationalizations for such practices, and, even if they are known to be untrue, they are nevertheless well found.

The very large amount of mental disorder, nervous tension, conflict, fear, anxiety, frustration, and insecurity which occurs in American society is largely due to the invariable failure of the false values by which men seek to live. The fact is that men cannot live in competition with one another without breaking down under the strain, however often they may attempt to relieve themselves of their frustrations and anxieties by attacking their scapegoats.

Man is born for co-operation, not for competition or conflict. This is a basic discovery of modern science. It confirms a discovery made some two thousand years ago by one Jesus of Nazareth. In a word: it is the principle of love which embraces within it all mankind. It is the principle of humanity, of one world, one brotherhood of peoples.

The measure of a person's humanity is the extent and intensity of his love for mankind. That measure is not the extent or intensity of his knowledge of the three R's. We all know to what a pass our knowledge of the three R's has brought us in a value system in which technology is esteemed far above humanity. We have been brought to, and we stand now upon, the very brink of destruction. If mankind is to be saved, it can be done only by replacing the values of industrial technology with those of humanity, of co-operation, of love. It is only when humanity is in control, that technology in the service of humanity will occupy its proper place in the scheme of things. A most important and immediate task is to make the people understand this. It is the duty of everyone capable of doing so to undertake this task. There must be a complete revaluation and reorientation of our values.

The school, beyond all else, must be considered as a place of education in the art and science of being a human being, the practice of human relations. Let us recall here the words of Franklin Delano Roosevelt from the 1945 Jefferson Day Speech which, so tragically, he did not live to deliver:

> ... the mere conquest of our enemies is not enough.
> We must go on to do all in our power to conquer the doubts and the fears, the ignorance and the greed which made this horror possible.
> Today, we are faced with the pre-eminent fact that *if civilization is to survive, we must cultivate the science of human relationships*—the ability of all peoples, of all kinds, to live together and work together in the same world at peace.

Without neglecting the important influence which the home constitutes, I believe that the science of human relationships is best taught and learned in the schools. We must shift the emphasis from the three R's to the fourth R, human relations, and place it first, foremost, and always in that order of importance, as the principal reason for the existence of the school. It must be clearly understood, once and for all time, that human relations are the most important of all relations. Upon this understanding must be based all our educational policies. We must train for humanity, and training in reading, writing, and arithmetic must be given in a manner calculated to serve the ends of that humanity. For all the knowledge in the world is worse than useless if it is not humanely understood and humanely used. An intelligence that is not humane is the most dangerous thing in the world.

Our schools must become institutions for the teaching of the most capitally important of all accomplishments, the theory and practice of human relations. Teachers must, therefore, be specially qualified to teach

137

human relations. The importance of their function must be recognized and suitably rewarded by a society anxious to encourage the entry of the best kind of people into the professional privilege of preparing human beings for the art of living. There can be no more important task than this. It is a task which demands qualities of the teacher of the highest order. He must be temperamentally fitted for his profession, and he should himself be an exemplar of the art of living and the practice of human relations. Children would learn more from such teachers than from all the factually informed instructors in the world.

MARIA MONTESSORI

Maria Montessori was born at Chiaravalle, near Ancona, Italy, on August 31, 1870. She studied at the University of Rome and was the first woman in Italy to receive an M.D. degree. While working in the university psychiatric clinic as an assistant physician she became interested in the education of mentally defective children. Such an interest caused her to start the Orthophrenic School for feeble-minded and defective children in 1898, utilizing the principles of Itard and Séguin. She served as principal of the school until 1900, and from 1900 to 1907 she lectured on pedagogy at the University of Rome.

In January 1907 Montessori established a nursery school (Casa dei Bambini) in the slum district of San Lorenzo, Rome. She established several other schools also, primarily for children from 3 to 6, and she directed these schools until 1911. From 1911 on she spent a great deal of the time touring the world explaining the ideas and methods she had discovered.

In 1922 she was named government inspector of schools in Italy, but the growing power of Mussolini's regime forced her to close all of the schools she had established. After World War II she made the Netherlands her permanent home, and Holland is today the world headquarters for the Montessori system. There are at the present time a number of Montessori schools in the United States and many leading universities provide instruction in the Montessori method.

Montessori wrote a number of books about education such as *The Montessori Method, Advanced Montessori Method, The Secret of Childhood, The Absorbent Mind, Spontaneous Activity in Education, The Discovery of the Child, Education for a New World*, and *To Educate the Human Potential*.

Montessori believes that we can know children by observing them, and she believes that too many educators interfere with a child's "spontaneous activity." Education, for Montessori, means removing barriers from the path which the child takes to discover the world. She believes that education should consist of a "prepared environment" with materials that children can utilize in ways that teach the child to learn.

THE SECRET OF CHILDHOOD

Maria Montessori

Till yesterday, till the beginning of the present century, society showed not the smallest concern for the child. It left him where he was born, to the sole care of his family. As his sole protection, there was the authority of the father, which is more or less a relic of that established by Roman Law over two thousand years ago. During so long a period of time, civilization evolved, changing its laws in favor and in the service of the adult, but it left the child without any social defense. To him were reserved only the material, moral or intellectual resources of the family into which he was born. And if in his family there were no such resources, the child had to develop in material, moral and intellectual indigence, without society's feeling the smallest responsibility for him. Society up till now has never claimed that the family should prepare itself in any way to receive and fittingly care for the children that might come to form part of it. The State, so rigorous in demanding official documents and meticulous preparations, and which so loves to regulate everything that bears the smallest trace of social responsibility, does not trouble to ascertain the capacity of future fathers to give adequate protection to their children or to guard their development. It has provided no place of instruction or preparation for parents. As far as the State is concerned, it is enough for anyone wishing to found a family to go through the marriage ceremony. In view of all this, we may well declare that society from earliest times has washed its hands of those little workers to whom nature has entrusted the task of building up humanity. In the midst of a continual progress in favor of the adult they have remained as beings

Maria Montessori. *The Secret of Childhood*, Longmans, Green and Company, New York, 1936, pp. 266-279.

not belonging to human society, extra-social, isolated, without any means of communication that would allow society to become aware of their condition. They might be victims, without society's being aware.

And in truth, they were victims.

Victims indeed, as science recognized, when about half a century ago medicine began to interest itself in childhood. At that time childhood was still more abandoned than today; there were neither child specialists nor children's hospitals. Statistics revealed so high a mortality during the first year of life that it caused a sensation. People began to reflect that though many children were born into families, few remained alive. The death of small children seemed so natural that families had accustomed themselves to it, comforting themselves with the thought that such little children went straight to heaven. There had come to be a special spiritual preparation teaching resigned submission to this kind of recruitment of little angels, whom, it was said, God wished to have near Him. Such vast numbers of babies died through ignorance or lack of proper care that the phenomenon was termed the constant slaughter of innocents.

The facts were made public and at once an extensive propaganda was begun to awaken human consciences to a new sense of responsibility. It was not enough for families to give life to their children, but they must save that life. And science showed how this could be done: fathers and mothers must gain new knowledge and receive the instruction necessary for a proper care of the health of their babies.

But it was not only in families that children suffered. Scientific investigations in the schools led to alarming revelations of torment. And this was in the last decade of the XIX Century—at a time when medicine was discovering and studying industrial diseases among workers, and showing the first steps to be taken for social hygiene in work. It was then perceived that besides infectious diseases resulting from unhygienic conditions, children too had their "industrial" diseases—the result of their work.

Their work lay in the schools. They were shut up there, slaves, exposed to the enforced torments of society. The narrow chest that brought an acquired predisposition to tuberculosis, came from long hours spent bending over desks, learning to read and write. The spinal column was curved through the same enforced position; eyes were short-sighted through the prolonged effort of trying to see without sufficient light.

The whole body was poisoned, as if it were asphyxiated, through long periods spent in small, closed spaces.

Yet their torment was not only physical; it extended to mental work. Studies were forced studies, and what with tedium and fear, the children's minds were tired, their nervous systems exhausted. They were lazy, discouraged, melancholic, vicious, with no faith in themselves, with none of the lovely gaiety of childhood.

Unhappy children! Oppressed children!

Their families realized nothing of all this. What concerned them was that their children should pass their examinations and learn their lessons as quickly as possible, so as to save time and money. It was not learning in itself, the attainment of a loftier culture that concerned the families, but the response to the summons of society, to the obligation imposed, an obligation which they found burdensome and which cost money. What was therefore important was that their sons should acquire their passport into the life of society in the shortest time possible.

Enquiries and investigations then carried out among school-children brought to light other startling facts. Many poor children when they came to school were already tired out by their morning's labors. Before going to school some of them had walked miles to distribute milk, or had gone running and shouting through the streets, selling newspapers, or had been working at home. They reached school hungry, sleepy, with the sole wish to rest. These poor little victims then received a larger share of punishments, for they could not pay attention to their teacher and so did not understand his explanations. And the teacher, concerned for his responsibility and still more for his authority, tried by punishments to awaken the interests of these worn out children and to drive them to obedience by threats. He would humiliate them before all their school-fellows, for incapacity or obstinacy. Such unfortunate children spent their lives exploited at home and punished at school.

The injustice revealed by these first investigations and enquiries was such that it led to a genuine social reaction. The schools and the relevant regulations were speedily modified. A new and important branch of medicine was inaugurated, covering School Health and exercising a protective and regenerating influence on all the official schools of civilized countries. Doctor and teacher were henceforth associated for the good of the pupils. This was, we may say, the first social sanction against an ancient unconscious error in the whole of humanity and it marked the first

143

step towards the social redemption of the child. If we look back to this initial awakening and follow the course of history, we shall find no salient fact revealing a recognition of the rights of the child, or an intuitive awareness of his importance. Christ alone called them to Him, pointing them out to adult man as his guides to the Kingdom of Heaven, and warning him of his blindness. But the adult continued to think only of converting the child, putting himself before him as example of perfection. It seemed as if this terrible blindness was incurable. Mystery of the human soul! This blindness has remained a universal phenomenon and is perhaps as old as mankind.[1]

In fact in every educational ideal, in all pedagogy up to our own time, the word education has been almost always synonymous with the word punishment. The end was always to subject the child to the adult, who substituted himself for nature, and set his reasoning and his end in the place of the laws of life. Different nations have different ways of punishing children. In private schools the punishments in use are often pointed out as they might point out their coat of arms. Some use humiliations, like tying placards to the children's backs, putting dunces' caps on their heads, or putting them in a real pillory so that those who pass can laugh at them and mock them. Children are put to stand in a corner for several hours, tired, bored by idleness, seeing nothing, but condemned to hold their position by their own will.

Other punishments are to make them kneel on stone floors with bare knees, or whipping, or public caning. A modern refinement of cruelty comes from the theory of associating school and family in the work of education—a principle which resolves itself into organizing school and family in inflicting punishment and tormenting the child. The child who is punished in school must consign his sentence to his father, so that the father may join with the teacher in punishing him and scolding. He is then forced to take back to school a writing from his father, as a proof that he has accused himself to his other executioner,

---

[1] It is tempting to make one more quotation from Alice Maynell. "*Tout passe.* Is the fruit for the flower, or the flower for the fruit, or the fruit for the seeds which it is formed to shelter and contain? It seems as though our forefathers had answered these questions most arbitrarily as to the life of man. . . .

"But impatience of the way and the wayfaring was to disappear from a later century—an age that has found all things to be on a journey, and all things complete in their day because it is their day, and has its appointed end. It is the tardy conviction of this, rather than a sentiment ready made, that has caused the childhood of children to seem, at last, something else than a defect."—*That Pretty Person.*

who associated himself, at least in principle, with the persecution of his own son. Thus the child is condemned to carry his own cross.

There is no one to defend him. Where is the tribunal to whom the child can appeal? It does not exist. Where is the love in which the child knows that he will find refuge and consolation? It is not there. School and family are agreed in punishing him, for if this were not so the punishment would be lessened and thus education would be abased.

But the family does not need reminders from school to punish its children. Investigations recently carried out on the punishments in use in families (and one such enquiry was carried out on the initiative of the educational institute attached to the League of Nations), show that even in our own time there is no country great or small in the world where children are not punished in their families. They are violently scolded, abused, beaten, slapped, kicked, driven out of sight, shut up in dark, frightening rooms, threatened with fantastic perils, or deprived of the little reliefs which are their refuge in their perpetual slavery or the solace of torments unconsciously endured, such as playing with their friends or eating sweets or fruit. And finally there is a family punishment of fasting inflicted usually in the evening, to go to bed without supper, so that, all night through, sleep is disturbed by grief and hunger.

Although among educated families punishments have rapidly diminished, they are still in use, and rough manners, a harsh, severe and threatening voice, are usual forms of behavior towards a child. It seems natural that the adults should have the right to beat the child, that his mother may slap him.

And yet arbitrary and public corporal punishment has been abolished for the adult. It would now lower his dignity and be a social disgrace. And yet what greater baseness can be conceived than that of insulting and persecuting a child? It is evident that the conscience of humanity lies buried in a deep sleep.

The progress of civilization today does not depend on individual progress, it does not spring from the burning flame of the human soul, it is the advance of an insensible machine, driven by an external force. The energy that moves it emanates from the outer world, like an immense impersonal power coming from society as a whole, and functioning inexorably. Forwards! Ever forwards!

Society is like a huge train travelling with a vertiginous velocity towards a distant point, while the individuals composing it are like travelers, asleep in their compartments. It is in that sleeping conscience that we find the mightiest obstacle to any vital aid or saving truth. If this were not so the world would be able to progress rapidly, there would not be the perilous contrast between the ever greater speed of material transport and the ever deeper-reaching rigidity of the human spirit. The first step, the most difficult in any social movement towards a collective progress, is the task of awakening this sleeping and insensible humanity and of forcing it to listen to the voice that calls it.

Today it is necessary that society as a whole should become aware of the child and of his importance, and that it should rapidly remedy the peril of the vast void on which it rests. It must fill that void by building the world for the child and recognizing his social rights. The greatest crime that society is committing is that of wasting the money it should spend for its children, of dissipating it to destroy them and itself. Society towards the child has acted like a guardian who dissipates the capital belonging to his ward. The adult world spends and makes for itself alone, whereas clearly a great part of its wealth should be destined for the child. This truth is inherent in life itself; the animals, the humblest insect, can teach it to us. For whom do the ants store up food? For whom do the bees suck nectar? For whom do the birds seek the food they carry to their nests? There is no example in nature of adults devouring everything themselves and leaving their offspring in want. Yet nothing is done for the human child; there is just the bare endeavor to preserve his body in a state of vegetative life. When wasteful society has urgent need of money, it takes it from the schools, and especially from the infant schools, that shelter the seeds of human life. It takes it from where there are neither arms nor voices to defend it. And therefore this is humanity's worst crime and greatest error. Society does not even perceive that it destroys twice over when it uses its money for instruments of destruction; it destroys by not enabling to live and it destroys by bringing death. And the two are one and the same error, for it is precisely through failing to assure the development of life that men have grown up in an abnormal manner.

Adults must now organize afresh and this time not for themselves but for their children. They must raise their voices to claim a right that they cannot see through their innate blindness, but which, once seen, is indisputable. If society has been a faithless guardian to the child, it must now make restitution of his goods and give him justice.

There is a mighty mission before all fathers. They alone can and must save their children, for they have the power to organize socially, and hence to act in the practice of associated life. Their consciences must feel the force of the mission entrusted to them by nature, a mission which sets them above society, which enables them to dominate all material circumstances, for in their hands lies positively the future of humanity, life.

If they will not do so, they will act like Pontius Pilate.

Pilate in Palestine was all-powerful, for he had the might of Rome behind him, the imperial power dominating all other powers.

Pilate could have saved Jesus. He could have, but he did not.

The mob with their ancient prejudices, the laws in force, custom, demanded the death of the innocent, the Redeemer, and Pilate remained undecided and inert.

"What can I do," he must have thought, "if these are the prevailing customs?"

And he washed his hands.

He had the power to say: "No, I will not!" But he did not say it.

Fathers today behave like Pilate, they abandon their children to social custom, which is so powerful as to seem a necessity.

And thus the social tragedy of the child takes its course. Society abandons the child, without feeling the smallest responsibility, to the care of his family, and the family, for its part, gives up the child to society which shuts him in school, isolating him from all family control.

Thus the child repeats the Passion of Christ, driven from Herod to Pilate, tossed between the two powers, who each leave Him to the responsibility of the other.

No voice is raised in the child's defense, and yet there is a voice that should have power to defend him, the voice of the blood, the power of life, the human authority of his father.

When the consciences of fathers awaken they will not act like Pilate, who to defend the Messiah denied His divinity, bound Him, scourged Him, and was the first to humiliate Him, saying "Ecce homo!"

This act history judges not as a defense of Christ, but as the first episode of His Passion.

ECCE HOMO

Yes, the child will pass through a passion, like the Passion of Christ.

But the beginning of all lies in that *Ecce Homo*. Behold the man. There is no God in him. He is empty, and he has been humiliated and beaten by the higher authority that could defend him.

After that he is dragged away by the crowd, by social authority. For the child the school has been a place of more than natural woe. Those big buildings seem made for a host of grown-up people, and everything is proportionate to the adult, the windows, the doors, the grey corridors, the bare, blank walls. There the child of many, many generations puts on the black uniform of mourning which would last through the whole period of childhood. On the threshold his family left him, for that door was forbidden them. Here was the separation of the two domains and the two responsibilities. And to the child, weeping and without hope, his heart shaken by fear, it was as if he read on the door Dante's inscription over the gates of Hell:

> Through me men go into the city of weeping,
> Through me men pass to the people of the lost.

It was a stern, threatening voice that summoned him to come in with other unknown companions, judged *en masse* as wicked creatures, who must be punished. Again Dante's verse comes to mind:

> "Woe unto you, evil souls."

Where will the child go?

He will go where he is ordered, where he is sent.

He has been judged. He will go into a class room, and someone will do as Dante's Minos, who, twisting his tail round his body, showed the lost soul to which circle it was destined. But everywhere there is eternal woe, with no escape.

When the child has gone in, into the class assigned to him, a teacher will *shut the door*. Henceforth she is mistress, she commands that group of souls, with no witness or control.

She will shut the door.

Family and society have surrendered their children to an authority. Men have scattered their own seed to the wind, and thither the wind has carried it. Henceforth those delicate, trembling limbs are held to the wood for more than three hours of anguish, three and three for many days, and months and years.

The child's hands and feet are fastened to the desk by stern looks, which hold them motionless as the nails of the Cross in the feet of Christ. The two little feet still and together, the two little hands joined and still, resting on the desk. And when into the mind athirst for truth and knowledge the ideas of the teacher are forcibly driven, as he wills, the little head humbled in submission will seem to bleed as by a crown of thorns.

The little heart so full of love will be pierced by the incomprehension of the world as by a sword. The culture offered to quench that thirst for knowledge will seem very bitter.

The tomb of the soul that was not able to live is already prepared, with all its camouflages, and when that soul is laid there, guards as though in mockery will be set round to see that it does not rise again.

But the child rises again, and returns, fresh and made anew, to live among men.

As Emerson says, the child is the eternal Messiah continually descending along fallen men, to lead them to the Kingdom of Heaven.

A. S. NEILL

A. S. Neill was born in Forfar, Scotland, on October 17, 1883. His father was a village schoolmaster and Neill was one of his pupils.

Neill entered Edinburgh University as a student of agricultural science when he was 25, but switched his major to English and received an M.A. in 1912. He later earned an M.Ed. with a specialization in psychology from Newcastle College.

Neill became headmaster of the Gretna Green School in Scotland where he taught boys and girls who would leave school at 14 to work on farms or in domestic service. He also taught at the King Alfred School in Hampstead, and in 1921 helped to set up an international school in the Helleran suburb of Dresden, Germany, called the Neue Schule. After several months of difficulties this school moved to Vienna, and then to Leiston, England, the present site of the Summerhill school.

Neill has written several books on education, including *Is Scotland Educated?*, *The Free Child, Talking of Summerhill, The Problem Child, Summerhill—A Radical Approach to Child Rearing*, and *Freedom—Not License.*

Neill believes that contemporary education is all wrong, and that it is too rigid and authoritarian. At Summerhill boys and girls are taught to be happy and well-adjusted, free of the restrictions, stupidities, fears, and lies of contemporary education. Neill believes that children are innately wise and realistic, and that if left free will develop as far as they are capable of developing. At Summerhill children are left free. They engage in activities they are interested in, and govern themselves.

SUMMERHILL

A. S. Neill

This is a story of a modern school—Summerhill.

Summerhill was founded in the year 1921. The school is situated within the village of Leiston, in Suffolk, England, and is about one hundred miles from London.

Just a word about Summerhill pupils. Some children come to Summerhill at the age of five years, and others as late as fifteen. The children generally remain at the school until they are sixteen years old. We generally have about twenty-five boys and twenty girls.

The children are divided into three age groups: The youngest range from five to seven, the intermediates from eight to ten, and the oldest from eleven to fifteen.

Generally we have a fairly large sprinkling of children from foreign countries. At the present time (1960) we have five Scandinavians, one Hollander, one German and one American.

The children are housed by age groups with a house mother for each group. The intermediates sleep in a stone building, the seniors sleep in huts. Only one or two older pupils have rooms for themselves. The boys live two or three or four to a room, and so do the girls. The pupils do not have to stand room inspection and no one picks up after them. They are left free. No one tells them what to wear: they put on any kind of costume they want to at any time.

Newspapers call it a *Go-as-you-please School* and imply that it is a gathering of wild primitives who know no law and have no manners.

It seems necessary, therefore, for me to write the story of Summerhill as honestly as I can. That I write with a bias is natural; yet I shall try to show the demerits of Summerhill as well as its merits. Its merits will be the merits of healthy, free children whose lives are unspoiled by fear and hate.

Obviously, a school that makes active children sit at desks studying mostly useless subjects is a bad school. It is a good school only for those who believe in *such* a school, for those uncreative citizens who want docile, uncreative children who will fit into a civilization whose standard of success is money.

Summerhill began as an experimental school. It is no longer such; it is now a demonstration school, for it demonstrates that freedom works.

When my first wife and I began the school, we had one main idea: *to make the school fit the child*—instead of making the child fit the school.

I had taught in ordinary schools for many years. I knew the other way well. I knew it was all wrong. It was wrong because it was based on an adult conception of what a child should be and of how a child should learn. The other way dated from the days when psychology was still an unknown science.

Well, we set out to make a school in which we should allow children freedom to be themselves. In order to do this, we had to renounce all discipline, all direction, all suggestion, all moral training, all religious instruction. We have been called brave, but it did not require courage. All it required was what we had—a complete belief in the child as a good, not an evil, being. For almost forty years, this belief in the goodness of the child has never wavered; it rather has become a final faith.

My view is that a child is innately wise and realistic. If left to himself without adult suggestion of any kind, he will develop as far as he is capable of developing. Logically, Summerhill is a place in which people who have the innate ability and wish to be scholars will be scholars; while those who are only fit to sweep the streets will sweep the streets. But we have not produced a street cleaner so far. Nor do I write this snobbishly, for I would rather see a school produce a happy street cleaner than a neurotic scholar.

What is Summerhill like? Well, for one thing, lessons are optional. Children can go to them or stay away from them—for years if they want to. There *is* a timetable—but only for the teachers.

The children have classes usually according to their age, but sometimes according to their interests. We have no new methods of teaching because we do not consider that teaching in itself matters very much. Whether a school has or has not a special method for teaching long division is of no significance, for long division is of no importance except to those who *want* to learn it. And the child who *wants* to learn long division *will* learn it no matter how it is taught.

Children who come to Summerhill as kindergarteners attend lessons from the beginning of their stay; but pupils from other schools vow that they will never attend any beastly lessons again at any time. They play and cycle and get in people's way, but they fight shy of lessons. This sometimes goes on for months. The recovery time is proportionate to the hatred their last school gave them. Our record case was a girl from a convent. She loafed for three years. The average period of recovery from lesson aversion is three months.

Strangers to this idea of freedom will be wondering what sort of madhouse it is where children play all day if they want to. Many an adult says, "If I had been sent to a school like that, I'd never have done a thing." Others say, "Such children will feel themselves heavily handicapped when they have to compete against children who have been made to learn."

I think of Jack who left us at the age of seventeen to go into an engineering factory. One day, the managing director sent for him.

"You are the lad from Summerhill," he said. "I'm curious to know how such an education appears to you now that you are mixing with lads from the old schools. Suppose you had to choose again, would you go to Eton or Summerhill?"

"Oh, Summerhill, of course," replied Jack.

"But what does it offer that the other schools don't offer?"

Jack scratched his head. "I dunno," he said slowly; "I think it gives you a feeling of complete self-confidence."

"Yes," said the manager dryly, "I noticed it when you came into the room."

"Lord," laughed Jack, "I'm sorry if I gave you that impression."

"I liked it," said the director. "Most men when I call them into the office fidget about and look uncomfortable. You came in as my equal. By the way, what department did you say you would like to transfer to?"

This story shows that learning in itself is not as important as personality and character. Jack failed in his university exams because he hated book learning. But his lack of knowledge about *Lamb's Essays* or the French language did not handicap him in life. He is now a successful engineer.

All the same, there is a lot of learning in Summerhill. Perhaps a group of our twelve-year-olds could not compete with a class of equal age in handwriting or spelling or fractions. But in an examination requiring originality, our lot would beat the others hollow.

We have no class examinations in the school, but sometimes I set an exam for fun. The following questions appeared in one such paper:

> *Where are the following:—Madrid, Thursday Island, yesterday, love, democracy, hate, my pocket screwdriver? (Alas, there was no helpful answer to that one.)*

> *Give meanings for the following: (the number shows how many are expected for each)—Hand (3) ... only two got the third right —the standard of measure for a horse. Brass (4) ... metal, cheek, top army officers, department of an orchestra. Translate Hamlet's To-be-or-not-to-be speech into Summerhillese.*

These questions are obviously not intended to be serious, and the children enjoy them thoroughly. Newcomers, on the whole, do not rise to the answering standard of pupils who have become acclimatized to the school. Not that they have less brain power, but rather because they have become so accustomed to work in a serious groove that any light touch puzzles them.

This is the play side of our teaching. In all classes much work is done. If, for some reason, a teacher cannot take his class on the appointed day, there is usually much disappointment for the pupils.

David, aged nine, had to be isolated for whooping cough. He cried bitterly. "I'll miss Roger's lesson in geography," he protested. David had been in the school practically from birth, and he had definite and final ideas about the necessity of having his lessons given to him. David is now a lecturer in mathematics at London University.

A few years ago someone at a General School Meeting (at which all school rules are voted by the entire school, each pupil and each staff member having one vote) proposed that a certain culprit should be punished by being banished from lessons for a week. The other children protested on the ground that the punishment was too severe.

My staff and I have a hearty hatred of all examinations. To us, the university exams are anathema. But we cannot refuse to teach children the required subjects. Obviously, as long as the exams are in existence, they are our master. Hence, the Summerhill staff is always qualified to teach to the set standard.

Not that many children want to take these exams; only those going to the university do so. And such children do not seem to find it especially hard to tackle these exams. They generally begin to work for them seriously at the age of fourteen, and they do the work in about three years. Of course they don't always pass at the first try. The more important fact is that they try again.

Summerhill is possibly the happiest school in the world. We have no truants and seldom a case of homesickness. We very rarely have fights—quarrels, of course, but seldom have I seen a stand-up fight like the ones we used to have as boys. I seldom hear a child cry, because children when free have much less hate to express than children who are downtrodden. Hate breeds hate, and love breeds love. Love means approving of children, and that is essential in any school. You can't be on the side of children if you punish them and storm at them. Summerhill is a school in which the child knows that he is approved of.

Mind you, we are not above and beyond human foibles. I spent weeks planting potatoes one spring, and when I found eight plants pulled up in June, I made a big fuss. Yet there was a difference between my fuss and that of an authoritarian. My fuss was about potatoes, but the fuss an authoritarian would have made would have dragged in the question of morality—right and wrong. I did not say that it was wrong to steal my spuds; I did not make it a matter of good and evil—I made it a matter of *my spuds*. They were *my* spuds and they should have been left alone. I hope I am making the distinction clear.

Let me put it another way. To the children, I am no authority to be feared. I am their equal, and the row I kick up about my spuds has no more significance to them than the row a boy may kick up about his punctured bicycle tire. It is quite safe to have a row with a child when you are equals.

Now some will say: "That's all bunk. There can't be equality. Neill is the boss; he is bigger and wiser." That is indeed true. I am the boss, and if the house caught fire the children would run to me. They know that I am bigger and more knowledgeable, but that does not matter when I meet them on their own ground, the potato patch, so to speak.

When Billy, aged five, told me to get out of his birthday party because I hadn't been invited, I went at once without hesitation—just as Billy gets out of my room when I don't want his company. It is not easy to describe this relationship between teacher and child, but every visitor to Summerhill knows what I mean when I say that the relationship is ideal. One sees it in the attitude to the staff in general. Rudd, the chemistry man, is Derek. Other members of the staff are known as Harry, and Ulla, and Pam. I am Neill, and the cook is Esther.

In Summerhill, everyone has equal rights. No one is allowed to walk on my grand piano, and I am not allowed to borrow a boy's cycle without his permission. At a General School Meeting, the vote of a child of six counts for as much as my vote does.

But, says the knowing one, in practice of course the voices of the grownups count. Doesn't the child of six wait to see how you vote before he raises his hand? I wish he sometimes would, for too many of my proposals are beaten. Free children are not easily influenced; the absence of fear accounts for this phenomenon. Indeed, the absence of fear is the finest thing that can happen to a child.

Our children do not fear our staff. One of the school rules is that after ten o'clock at night there shall be quietness on the upper corridor. One night, about eleven, a pillow fight was going on, and I left my desk, where I was writing, to protest against the row. As I got upstairs, there was a scurrying of feet and the corridor was empty and quiet. Suddenly I heard a disappointed voice say, "Humph, it's only Neill," and the fun began again at once. When I explained that I was trying to write a book downstairs, they showed concern and at once agreed to chuck the noise. Their scurrying came from the suspicion that their bedtime officer (one of their own age) was on their track.

I emphasize the importance of this absence of fear of adults. A child of nine will come and tell me he has broken a window with a ball. He tells me, because he isn't afraid of arousing wrath or moral indignation. He may have to pay for the window, but he doesn't have to fear being lectured or being punished.

There was a time some years back when the School Government resigned, and no one would stand for election. I seized the opportunity of putting up a notice: "In the absence of a government, I herewith declare myself Dictator. Heil Neill!" Soon there were mutterings. In the afternoon Vivien, aged six, came to me and said, "Neill, I've broken a window in the gym."

I waved him away. "Don't bother me with little things like that," I said, and he went.

A little later he came back and said he had broken two windows. By this time I was curious, and asked him what the great idea was.

"I don't like dictators," he said, "and I don't like going without my grub." (I discovered later that the opposition to dictatorship had tried to take itself out on the cook, who promptly shut up the kitchen and went home.)

"Well," I asked, "what are you going to do about it?"

"Break more windows," he said doggedly.

"Carry on," I said, and he carried on.

When he returned, he announced that he had broken seventeen windows. "But mind," he said earnestly, "I'm going to pay for them." "How?"

"Out of my pocket money. How long will it take me?"

I did a rapid calculation. "About ten years," I said.

He looked glum for a minute; then I saw his face light up. "Gee," he cried, "I don't have to pay for them at all."

"But what about the private property rule?" I asked. "The windows are my private property."

"I know that but there isn't any private property rule now. There isn't any government, and the government makes the rules."

It may have been my expression that made him add, "But all the same I'll pay for them."

But he didn't have to pay for them. Lecturing in London shortly afterward, I told the story; and at the end of my talk, a young man came up and handed me a pound note "to pay for the young devil's windows." Two years later, Vivien was still telling people of his windows and of the man who paid for them. "He must have been a terrible fool, because he never even saw me."

Children make contact with strangers more easily when fear is unknown to them. English reserve is, at bottom, really fear; and that is why the most reserved are those who have the most wealth. The fact that Summerhill children are so exceptionally friendly to visitors and strangers is a source of pride to me and my staff.

We must confess, however, that many of our visitors are people of interest to the children. The kind of visitor most unwelcome to them is the teacher, especially the earnest teacher, who wants to see their drawing and written work. The most welcome visitor is the one who has good tales to tell—of adventure and travel or, best of all, of aviation. A boxer or a good tennis player is surrounded at once, but visitors who spout theory are left severely alone.

The most frequent remark that visitors make is that they cannot tell who is staff and who is pupil. It is true: the feeling of unity is that strong when children are approved of. There is no deference to a teacher as a teacher. Staff and pupils have the same food and have to obey the same community laws. The children would resent any special privileges given to the staff.

When I used to give the staff a talk on psychology every week, there was a muttering that it wasn't fair. I changed the plan and made the talks open to everyone over twelve. Every Tuesday night, my room is filled with eager youngsters who not only listen but give their opinions freely. Among the subjects the children have asked me to talk about have been these: The Inferiority Complex, The Psychology of Stealing, The Psychology of the Gangster, The Psychology of Humor, Why Did Man Become a Moralist?, Masturbation, Crowd Psychology. It is obvious that such children will go out into life with a broad clear knowledge of themselves and others.

The most frequent question asked by Summerhill visitors is, "Won't the child turn round and blame the school for not making him learn arithmetic or music?" The answer is that young Freddy Beethoven and young Tommy Einstein will refuse to be kept away from their respective spheres.

The function of the child is to live his own life—not the life that his anxious parents think he should live, nor a life according to the purpose of the educator who thinks he knows what is best. All this interference and guidance on the part of adults only produces a generation of robots.

You cannot *make* children learn music or anything else without to some degree converting them into will-less adults. You fashion them into accepters of the *status quo*—a good thing for a society that needs obedient sitters at dreary desks, standers in shops, mechanical catchers of the 8:30 suburban train—a society, in short, that is carried on the shabby shoulders of the scared little man—the scared-to-death conformist.

MAX RAFFERTY

Max Rafferty was born on May 7, 1917, in New Orleans, Louisiana. He graduated from Beverly Hills High School in 1933, and went on to obtain a B.A. degree in history at the University of California in Los Angeles in 1938. He obtained an M.A. in 1949, and an Ed.D. in school administration in 1955. He has since received honorary degrees from Lincoln University and Brigham Young University.

Rafferty has been a teacher, principal, and athletic director. He became district superintendent of the Saticoy Elementary School District in 1951 and served there until 1955, then in the Needles Elementary and High School Districts from 1955 to 1961, and in the La Canada District from 1961 to 1962. In 1962 he was elected as California's State Superintendent of Public Instruction, and reelected to this post in 1966.

Rafferty has received national recognition for his work in education, and was honored with the Shankland Memorial Award of the American Association of School Administrators. He has achieved a reputation as an orator, and also as a writer. He has written *Practices and Trends in School Administration, Suffer Little Children,* and *What Are They Doing to Your Children?* Rafferty also writes "The Dr. Max Rafferty Column" which is printed in many newspapers around the country.

Rafferty has long been associated with conservative forces in education and politics, and has been a long-time foe of Progressive education. Rafferty has argued for what he calls "education in depth" and has been opposed to "life adjustment" in education, as well as to "frills" which he feels Progressive education promotes. Rafferty strongly supports a program of education that would promote the three R's, as well as religion and patriotism in education.

WHAT ARE THEY DOING TO YOUR CHILDREN?

Max Rafferty

Every profession has its own symbolism and its own emblem.

Law has its blindfold and carefully balanced scales; medicine its caduceus, the rod and serpents; theology the Cross of Christ or the Star of David.

Education alone has always had as its emblem an entity as elusive and ever-changing as itself—the flickering, fragile flame. Whether flaring from the torch or glowing sedately from the lamp, fire has traditionally been the symbol of the learning process.

There is far more than mere chance bound up in this. Ages ago, we are told, when the world was young and man toed impatiently the starting blocks that marked the beginning of the long and perilous race from Yesterday to Today, a great gift came somehow into his keeping. Before it came, man struggled grimly for mere existence, a puny, frightened underdog in a world where tusk and claw were the key to survival and where the entire human species numbered but a scant few thousand members, harassed and hunted by the powerful and savage beasts that haunted the dark forests and scoured the vast plains of primeval Earth.

But the coming of the gift of fire changed everything. It set Homo sapiens apart, forever and completely, from the swarming multitudes of species that inhabited the planet. The old Greeks said that Prometheus stole it from the gods themselves and willingly condemned himself to everlasting pain that man might rule the world. A score of civiliza-

Max Rafferty. *What Are They Doing to Your Children?* The New American Library, Inc., New York, 1963, pp. 11-18. © 1963 by Max Rafferty and reprinted by permission.

tions hailed fire as divine and worshipped it accordingly. It blazed upon uncounted altars and brightened the rituals of a hundred faiths.

And indeed fire bore within itself a potent magic. Sparkling and strange, impossible to hold, yet dangerous to do without, equally likely to be the comforter of the cheery hearthside and the destroyer of the house, fire presented man with a whole new set of challenges. As perhaps nothing else, before or since, it forced him to think in different terms.

In this connection, a story is told of the famous political economist, John Stuart Mill. It seems that he was tormented for weeks on end by a dream. It was not a nightmare or even the unpleasant aftermath of overdone Welsh rarebit or underdone mutton. It was simply that the great man woke up every morning with the unshakable conviction that at some time during the still, small watches of the preceding night he had had revealed to him the answer to the riddle of the universe. His problem was that he could never manage to remember the next morning what the answer had been. He retained merely the tantalizing knowledge that the answer had indeed been given to him.

At last the great philosopher could stand it no longer. He armed himself before retiring with a pen and paper, placed on a special stand beside the bed. He repeated grimly, over and over again as he was dropping off to sleep, the single phrase "*I will* wake up, *I will* wake up!" And finally one night the powerful mind of John Stuart Mill snapped the velvet bonds of Morpheus and brought himself bolt upright in his bed, drugged with slumber but muttering the words of Archimedes: "I have found it!"

His shaking hand seized the nearby pen and scrawled a single sentence upon the paper placed there on purpose to receive the Secret of the Ages. Then, exhausted by this supreme effort of will, Mill lay back upon his pillow and went promptly back to sleep. The next morning he remembered his nocturnal triumph and hastened to read the magic formula that alone could solve all the problems of mankind. Upon the paper were written four short words: "Think in different terms."

It was this lesson that fire taught to man. With it he forged the weapons with which he conquered first the brute world about him and later the vastly greater inner world of Nature herself.

Education is strangely similar. Forced into a rigid authoritarian mold, it changes shape and form like fire itself and escapes into the free outer air. Like fire, too, education compels man to think in unaccustomed ways and places in his hands undreamed-of tools with which to shape his own destiny.

The parallel does not stop here, however. When Troy burned, fire was used to put an end to years of blind passion and unreason. The burning of Rome destroyed a city dedicated to unlimited tyranny over all men everywhere. And the Great Fire of London occurred at the height of an age of ignorance, squalor, and superstition.

Is not education similarly bound to wage eternal war against the same evils? If we educators do not find the justification for our life work in fighting unreason and tyranny and superstition, then how indeed are we to vindicate our ancient calling?

It seems to me that my profession needs to revive its immemorial relationship with fire. This means that just as man was forced to explore the nature of fire in order to arrive at its ultimate meaning for the human race, so also must we now proceed to an examination of the nature of education.

It used to be like Home and Mother, you know—non-controversial. Any politician could get an easy round of applause just by putting in a good word for the schools, and a legislator who voted against an education bill was lumped in the same category as one who went home every night and beat his wife.

Things have changed of late. Since Sputnik, it has become fashionable to use the nation's schools as a whipping boy for all sorts of sins and offenses, real or imaginary. Today there boils and bubbles throughout the land a great debate in regard to education—its character and its cost, its follies and its finenesses, its facts and its fictions. Above all, there is an absorbing interest in the proper role of education in the second half of the twentieth century. Perhaps if we could reach a consensus on this question, we would be better able to chart the course of education's future.

But right here we run into trouble. Agreement on education is as hard to come by as is agreement on international disarmament. We can't even agree on its definition and characteristics.

Webster says education is the imparting of knowledge and skill, especially through systematic instruction or training.

John Dewey characterized it as enabling its possessor to the other world.

Aristotle said that education is what makes men good.

Socrates said it is the only thing the soul takes with her to the other world.

Diogenes Laërtius called it an ornament in prosperity and a refuge in adversity.

Huxley described it as the ability to make one do the thing he has to do, when it ought to be done, whether he likes it or not.

Arthur Guiterman said simply: "Education is making men."

Trevelyan, who was somewhat cynical, commented that education has produced a vast population able to read but unable to distinguish what is worth reading.

And Robert Hutchins, who is downright pessimistic, admits in part that we don't know what education is because we have never really tried it.

These numerous and contradictory definitions and characterizations tend to cancel each other out, and leave us still seeking one helpful signpost in this forest of authorities. Yet, despite the semantic difficulties posed by the question "What is education?" the country is in dire need of an answer upon which most citizens, both lay and professional, can reach an agreement. Such an agreement does not now exist, even among the educators. But for centuries—in fact, up until about 1930—a consensus did actually exist among the great majority of informed and interested people as to what the goals of education should be.

Cardinal Newman summarized these as "raising the intellectual tone of society, cultivating the public mind, purifying the national taste, giving enlargement and sobriety to the ideas of the age, facilitating the exercise of political power, and refining the intercourse of private life." When Newman described the educated man as "having a gift which serves him in public and supports him in retirement, without which good fortune is but vulgar, and with which failure and disappointment have a certain charm," he was expressing the culminating aspirations of two thousand years of Western civilization. Education to Newman and his contemporaries was something tangible, a commodity that, like a torch, could be passed from one generation to the next. The teacher was the torchbearer.

But to John Dewey and his followers, education was life adjustment. These men, and the philosophy that came to be known, unfortunately, as progressive education, drew strength from a strange combination of circumstances and events: a general reaction against the sterile classicism of the late nineteenth century, the breakdown of discipline and moral standards after World War I, the unprecedented demands and stresses posed by universal education, and finally the world-wide rise of totalitarianism.

Of all the authorities who have taken the trouble to analyze the phenomenal spread in the country during the thirties and forties of progressive education, none to my knowledge has bothered to trace the deadly parallel between this philosophy and that of the great dictators who rose and flourished during this same era.

When Dewey and his "instrumentalism" said that there were no eternal truths, he was saying that no particular subject matter was vital to the educated man, and—as a logical consequence—no God either. And this was exactly what the dictators were saying to their enslaved people.

When George Counts and his credo of collectivism downgraded the individual and described him as important only as a member of his "peer group," he was right up Hitler's and Mussolini's alley.

When William Heard Kilpatrick with his "pragmatism" denounced learning for the sake of learning and listed "life adjustment" as the supreme goal of education, he was discouraging nonconformity precisely as was Stalin.

And when Harold Rugg glorified the principles of socialism in the name of better textbooks for America's children, he was attempting, knowingly or unknowingly, to start this country down the same bad old road to totalitarianism along which Germany and Italy and Japan and Russia were already traveling.

When the progressive educationists asked the rhetorical question "Dare the schools build a new social order?" the order they were talking about was always some sort of state socialism.

Progressive education warred on competition.

It rejected graded, subject-matter report cards.

It frowned on classroom ability groupings.

It refused to retain pupils in one grade even if the pupils in turn had declined to make any effort to go on to the next grade.

All this was done in the name of democracy. "Democracy in Education" became in fact the watchword of the new philosophy, a semantic gambit typical of the totalitarians, who always say "peace" when they mean "war," "black" when they mean "white," and "democracy" when they mean exactly the opposite.

Wherever progressive education was allowed to infiltrate—and this was almost everywhere—the mastery of basic skills began insensibly to erode, knowledge of the great cultures and contributions of past civilizations started to slip and slide, reverence for the heroes of our nation's past faded and withered under the burning glare of pragmatism. In the place of these mighty building blocks of education, which had buttressed and bulwarked instruction for centuries, we substituted such airy and ephemeral soap bubbles as "group dynamics," "social living," and "orientation." In many places, even the alphabet was forbidden to the children, and the schools taught reading in a manner unknown since the days of the ancient Egyptians, by having the boys and girls draw "pictures" of words and memorize them.

The beginning of national revulsion against this cult first became noticeable the day after Sputnik started riding the world's skyspace. It picked up speed with Dr. James B. Conant's quiet but devastating critique of secondary education a year or so later. The trend is irreversible, and plain to those with eyes to see.

One major implication of the new trend in education is that of a better break for the classroom teacher. At present there is a definite rift between the professional educator and the lay public. There is no blinking the fact that in America the teacher simply does not enjoy the prestige and status which in other countries is accorded the practitioner of the ancient and honorable art of education.

The story may be apocryphal, but one of my former students swears he witnessed a Parisian gendarme stopping traffic to escort a robed professor of the Sorbonne across a busy thoroughfare. This is status with a vengeance. In our country the professor is more likely to end up getting run down. The reason for this is that within the last generation in this nation the teacher and the parents have developed different sets of educational values.

Parents, by and large, want what they have always wanted for their children. They want them turned into civilized patriotic citizens speaking and writing good English; able to succeed both in business and college; possessing at least a passable knowledge of our great cultural heritage; trained in such minimum essentials as reading, basic mathematics, spelling, grammar, history, and geography; and, above all, well enough grounded in habits of diligence, perseverance, and orderly thinking to enable them to prepare for adult life. For even the humblest parent recognizes instinctively today that it is going to be absolutely necessary for his children and grandchildren to be well educated in the world of tomorrow.

But for the past thirty years, teachers have been told by those responsible for their training and accreditation that none of these things were of any great importance at all. It has become increasingly difficult to teach patriotism to children without being accused of "indoctrinating" them, despite the undoubted fact that every generation of Americans has taught such patriotism to its children for almost two hundred years without the slightest questioning or soul-searching.

Good English has become increasingly ignored as its standards have been imperceptibly diluted by a philosophy that held that it didn't make much difference how a child said something so long as he could make himself understood, that it was somehow authoritarian to impose a so-called "middle-middle-class" speech pattern upon an "upper-lower-class" child, that analyzing sentences and conjugating verbs and recognizing dangling participles were stultifying to the child's creative urge, and that if the child's "peer group" spoke miserable English it might be best for the school not to insist upon too high speech standards for the individual pupil lest—horror of horrors—he be "rejected" by his more colloquial and less literate peers.

History and geography were summarily lumped together with civics and economics into a synthetic catchall labeled "social studies" or in some places "social living," and so it has gone. The profession has managed to get badly out of step with the rest of the American people.

Surely if education is to have a future, it must reflect the ideals of the great public that supports and populates the schools. When our professional leaders decide to give the children the kind of an education their parents want those children to get, it is going to mark a whole new era in teacher-parent relationships. The teacher will be respected then because he is a learned and scholarly professional, a master of organized subject matter, and above all an expert in teaching children to think in a systematic manner. There will be little public resistance then to paying good salaries to subject-matter specialists. There is considerable resistance right now to paying high salaries to the specialists in "togetherness," "ingroupness," and "life adjustment."

I am sure that relatively soon there is going to be a consensus on what education really is. You will note that some pages back I started trying to reach a definition of education and that the pursuit of this elusive goal has led me all around Robin Hood's barn. To go at one jump from the ridiculous to the sublime, it should perhaps be noted that a similar attempt by Plato to define the word "justice" led him in the end to write an entire book upon the subject of the ideal state. He found that justice could exist only when the surrounding climate was prepared to receive and support it.

Exactly so is the case of education. Only when the vast bulk of the citizens who make up this country can reach a basic agreement on what they want their schools to do can education be properly and lastingly defined. As a result of recent far-reaching events and changes in popular thinking, we are nearer to such an agreement than we have been for more than a generation. My own choice of a definition is that of Josiah Royce: "Education is learning to use the tools which the race has found indispensable." In too many places still, where teachers are taught to teach, this sentiment has been junked in favor of the progressive educationists' "Education is the happy, comfortable adjustment of the child to his peer group."

Properly understood and utilized, Royce's definition can bring all of us together—professional and layman, parent and teacher. We can go forward with confidence, rejecting the theory that calls for teaching to the lowest common denominator, the absence of positive standards, the glorification of group acceptance as the supreme goal. We can proclaim instead that certain things in this world and this life are lastingly important; that education exists to uphold and to sow widespread in the minds and hearts of men the good, the true, and the beautiful; and that there is still a brightly glowing torch to be handed down through the schools from one generation to the next, unto the very end of time.

H. G. RICKOVER

H. G. Rickover was born in Tsarist Russia on January 27, 1900. His parents migrated to the United States in 1906 and settled in Chicago. He attended John Marshall High School in Chicago, and after graduation was appointed to the United States Naval Academy. He was commissioned an ensign in 1922. After serving for five years in the Navy he returned to the Naval Academy to study electrical engineering at the postgraduate level. He continued his work in this field at Columbia University, and received an M.S. in electrical engineering in 1929.

Rickover served in several different naval posts, and in 1945 became Inspector General of the Nineteenth Fleet. He left this post to serve as Assistant Director of Operations at the Atomic Energy Commission's Manhattan Project at Oak Ridge, Tennessee, where he planned and supervised the construction of the first atomic submarine, the Nautilus. He is often heralded as the "father of the atomic submarine," and in 1959 he was advanced to the rank of vice admiral.

Rickover has written a number of books about education, including *American Education—A National Failure, Education and Freedom,* as well as *Swiss Schools and Ours.*

Rickover has received national attention as an outspoken critic of American education. He feels that our schools are inadequate in many ways, particularly in the teaching of mathematics and science. Rickover decries our lack of national standards, and believes that too much of American education is either repetitious or consists of large gaps in learning. He holds the Swiss educational system in high esteem and believes that we should emulate many of their practices.

EDUCATION AND FREEDOM

H. G. Rickover

The powerful thrust of Sputnik's launching device did more than penetrate outer space. It also pierced the thick armor encasing our complacent faith in America's present and future technological supremacy. It blasted the comfortable conviction that only in an atmosphere of personal independence and political liberty can science and scientists flourish. It shook the belief, long taken for granted, that a high standard of material well-being is both the outward manifestation and the necessary basis for technological progress.

It did greatest damage to our trust in the American educational system—up to now almost as sacrosanct as motherhood. Harsh words are being said about its methods no less than about its aims. Sputnik has been seen as a triumph of Russian education, and rightly so. Reams of words and figures have filled the newspaper columns describing Russian education, comparing it with ours, and trying to pinpoint where we have failed in the vital educational task of motivating and training the skilled professionals needed by our country while Russia seems to have no trouble turning them out in vast numbers.

We are asking searching questions about the aims of education in a modern technological society and how our schools can best achieve them. We are finally coming out of our traditional educational isolation and looking at the educational systems of other countries of Western civilization in order to compare them with ours. But we are still not ready to do this in a spirit of detachment, as I shall show later. The whole reappraisal has been painful but good for us.

Sputnik may well be the catalyst which brings about drastic and long-overdue reforms in utilizing the nation's intellectual resources. It may thus do in matters of the intellect what Pearl Harbor did in matters industrial and military. Then, as now, a dramatic occurrence suddenly revealed that we had failed to develop our capacities to their maximum potential. As we found then that in a national emergency we could take prompt and vigorous action and perform industrial miracles, so I am convinced we can now take similar action and perform educational miracles.

Let us not lose our heads and despair of American technological competence *as it is today*. The real danger lies somewhat in the future and can be averted if we will act. At the moment, I for one am convinced that we have the men and the resources which, if properly directed and given priority, could have put a satellite in orbit ahead of the Russians. This, of course, is no excuse for our mistake in letting Russia win a propaganda victory, damaging to our prestige among uncommitted nations of the world and, it is to be feared, also among some of our friends.

The Sputnik was aloft first, and that is regrettable. What is particularly regrettable is that to many people it looks not like a military weapon but like pure, scientific adventure of a kind which appeals to their imagination as no superior weapon could. Russia indeed chose shrewdly where to concentrate for a blow to our scientific and technological prestige. It also fits nicely into the International Geophysical Year. In actual fact, Sputnik is of course of great military significance because of its relation to missile weaponry and because of the potential military advantages of outer-space control.

The successful Russian satellite program brings out two important facts which we would disregard at our peril: *First*, it demonstrates conclusively that a modern totalitarian state can depress the standard of living of its people to the level of the most backward countries while simultaneously raising a limited sector of the economy to a standard as high as, if not higher than, comparable sectors of the economy of the most highly developed country in the world. Theoretically, the favored sector could be any one chosen as of greatest national importance by the rulers of a totalitarian state; in practice it will inevitably be the sector which significantly benefits the country's military and political power. *Second*, it proves that a modern despotism can

174

devise an educational system shaped solely in the interest of the state and in complete disregard of the needs of the individual child, and yet induce *all* children to stretch their intellectual capacities to the utmost. These factors are worth examining in more detail.

We are of course familiar with the total power exercised by the self-chosen rulers of modern totalitarian states. We have known that they could and did manipulate the productive capacity of their countries in a way which puts heavy industry and armaments production ahead of production of consumer goods. But most of us felt that in the long run they would be forced to strike a better balance. I believe we must now accept as fact a permanent imbalance, probably of increasing proportion, between the civilian and the politico-military sector of the Russian economy. The very backwardness of the civilian sector, far from hampering progress, is proving an advantage to Russia's rulers.

Unrest in Soviet-dominated countries, where communism is a foreign importation, which brought with it a steep decline in the economic well-being of the people and deterioration in their spiritual life, does not mean that similar unrest will necessarily appear in Russia herself. What must not be forgotten is that almost everyone who had enjoyed material well-being under the old Russian regime was killed or driven out. The rest of the people have never known greater material benefits or more political freedom than they are now permitted to enjoy. If anything, they live better. Though they do not have so much milk or meat as in pre-revolutionary days, they now have something which gives greater satisfaction to a people from whom the world of books, of ideas, of music, and art had for centuries been withheld. They have a chance at an education, limited and utilitarian as it may be; they have greater opportunities to see a show, a ballet, to hear concert music, even if they must queue up for hours to obtain tickets. Measured against the past, the Russian standard of living is not in itself low enough to cause unrest, and comparison with life in other countries is carefully prevented.

Authoritarian control and the low standard of living make the running of the civilian sector simple and cheap. It takes less time, effort, and money to issue orders and deaden independent thought by propaganda than to seek consent by marshaling convincing arguments and winning free-and-open discussions. The cost in time and money of the whole paraphernalia of parliamentary or congressional government is eliminated. Cost of mass media can be kept at a fraction of what is customary in free countries, and the personnel required need be neither so numerous nor so competent.

The entire business complex is missing and in its place there is a weak consumer-industries sector which merely has to keep people reasonably warm, adequately fed, and provided with a roof over their heads. There is no need for attractive stores, for service industries, for advertising. Almost the whole automobile complex is lacking. No chain of garages, auto dealers, service stations, etc. All that are needed are trucks and a few cars for the elite. One could go on *ad finitum*.

Obviously, given similar resources in land and population, the modern totalitarian state can put into the politico-military sector many times as much wealth and man power as a democratic country. With the same number of scientists and engineers concentrating on a few projects deemed of great national importance, spectacular technological breakthroughs can be achieved. Moreover, the meager demands of the civilian economy on irreplaceable mineral and fuel resources prevent rapid deterioration of the country's resources base such as now threatens all highly developed countries. When all the gasoline has been burned up by the American family car, Russia may still have a reserve in the ground for her planes, submarines, and tanks.

All non-totalitarian countries are multiple-purpose societies in which national income as well as national wealth and man power is allocated to different sectors of the economy under the price system of the open market. Even where democracy is but a feeble force, governments are in practice not free to dispose arbitrarily of people and property except in time of war. In our country, as in all countries of Western civilization, it is the value judgments of the average man which determine how the country's man power and productive capacity are to be utilized. I believe that everywhere the average man makes decisions by judging how they would affect, first, himself and his family; second, the group with which he is most closely associated—neighborhood, political party, religious, professional, or ethnical group; and last the nation as a whole. For some few there is a fourth category—the world.

This order of values is often self-defeating. A man may feel that his personal interest in tax reduction outweighs the importance of good public education; or he may feel that the money his firm can save by letting industrial wastes pollute a river outweighs the interest of the community in preserving aesthetic values, natural beauty, and a pure water supply; or that he has the right to use pressure tactics to increase his income even if this will result in inflation. He may feel that he has a better right to the biggest, heaviest automobile than the nation has to conserve a dwindling stock of irreplaceable minerals and fuels; he would like the country's foreign policy to favor his parents' country of origin whether this is to the advantage of our country as a whole or not. Re-examination of such judgments will often show that they have actually done more harm to the narrower interests than would have a decision which puts wider interests first.

In our country the major share of all our technical effort has gone into spreading ever higher standards of material well-being over ever larger segments of the population. Perhaps too large an effort has gone into the things that make American life pleasant and comfortable and not enough into the things that insure continuous spiritual and material growth as well as military and political victory in any war, hot or cold.

In the long run, the more disturbing fact which is disclosed by the Russian satellite program is Russia's success in building in record time an educational system which produces exactly the sort of trained men and women her rulers need to achieve technological supremacy the day after tomorrow. Russian education is, of course, deplorably utilitarian and authoritarian. However, it has virtually wiped out illiteracy; today estimated to be only 2.5 to 5 per cent, which does not compare badly with our own rate—3.7 per cent in 1940 and about 2.5 per cent today. Russia has put a *larger* percentage of her *smaller* national income into public education than the United States. She has made the rewards of intellectual accomplishment so attractive that her children are working extremely hard to keep up with a tough curriculum. Russia has as great a shortage as we in school buildings—she merely doubles up and so gets twice the benefit we do out of each classroom and school laboratory. I feel sure she would use her schools on a three-shift basis if this were necessary. Russia has no teacher shortage, no sub-standard teachers—she has set their scholastic standards high and gives them a heavy work load, but she also honors them and pays them well. Russia evidently has no difficulty getting intelligent people with solid education in their chosen subjects to work devotedly and without worrying too much about lack of political freedom. This has been a surprise to us—an unpleasant surprise.

Had we looked at the matter from the point of view of the peasant children earnestly studying in classroom, laboratory, and library we would not have been so surprised. The low standard of living and the memory of a past, meager in culture, are assets to the Soviets. It is difficult for us to understand the intense longing for education—any kind of education—of underdeveloped people. This is a strong bond that unites Russia—no longer underdeveloped but close enough to the immediate backward past—with all the underdeveloped people of the world.

Moreover, it is far easier to awaken in children a sense of personal achievement, of victory, in mastering the intellectual challenge of tough curricula, if there are no competing attractions such as those which claim the attention of our more fortunate children: no comfortable home, playrooms, and back yards to play in; no juke boxes; far fewer movies; hardly any distracting radio or TV programs; no senior proms, dating, long telephone conversations; and of course no hot rods. If they could have them, these pleasant things would greatly delight Russia's youngsters and probably cut into their study time; witness their avid interest in American jive and rock-'n-roll records—to the dismay of the authorities. Russia does have a problem with unruly so-called young hooligans who are—and this is significant—not the children of the poor, but the pampered offspring of Russia's elite. Eventually there may be more of these disturbing youths, but for the moment they hardly make a dent in the picture of an earnest, well-disciplined, polite, and studious school population.

It has surprised us to find that Russia's intellectual elite does highly competent work despite authoritarian control in all—even the highest—educational and research institutions. Russia appears to have found a way of allowing superior minds freedom in the field of their special competence while denying them the right of political criticism. It has apparently been possible to develop the critical capacity of superior minds to the high degree needed for scientific work while fettering it in all other fields. There is evidence that the fetters are well hidden, and that discontent with Russian life is largely prevented. This seems to be done by shrewdly catering to the needs of these people both as scientists and as ordinary men and women. They are allowed to let their minds roam undisturbed in quest of knowledge; they are given superb laboratory and research facilities; the best thoughts of foreign

178

scientists are gathered quickly from scientific magazines and books the world over and presented by large staffs of abstracters to any Russian scientist who needs them; honors are heaped on scientists and engineers for superior achievements although they do not so often get their names in the papers as do their colleagues in the free world, for this would smack of "personality cult."

Scientists also have needs of the kind common to all mortals, so Russia gives them attractive living quarters, country houses, vacations, maids, cars, and chauffeurs. Their pay is in the top-income bracket; in fact, the highest salary in Russia is paid to the president of the Soviet Academy of Sciences. Why should these men concern themselves about the lack of political freedom or the grim and dreary life of most of their compatriots? They probably reason that these are temporary abuses and that their own scientific work will contribute to the wealth and power of their country and thus ultimately to a better life for everyone. Quite possibly, too, totalitarian states may have a built-in incentive for attracting gifted minds to science: the desire to escape from the grim reality of life to a safe and comfortable ivory tower.

It is an unfortunate accident of history for us that today the military and political power of a country depends so largely on having a highly developed technical civilization. This, in turn, calls for vast numbers of scientists and engineers. The subjects which these men must master are mathematics, physics, chemistry, astronomy—all apparently regarded as politically safe by Russia's rulers. Even the most fanatic Marxist would have trouble interjecting the party line into these particular sciences. It is different, however, with other sciences. Take biology: this is a science which heretofore could not be freely pursued in Russia. Scientific truth had to be sacrificed to the Lysenko-Stalin theory of genetics. Other than party-line limitations may also restrict free scientific inquiry. For example, Russia does not presently consider it necessary to excel in medical research. Chemists are therefore diverted from inquiries which might cure diseases of man to inquiries which can improve metals. The results of costly foreign medical research are instantly available to Russia so she can shift appropriations from the medical to the engineering faculty and save money and man power.

Enough has been said to give an inkling of the methods by which the Soviet manipulates its skilled man power. It might be noted in passing that the fields in which they have done outstanding work have been precisely those where they allowed maximum intellectual freedom. Little that is new and original has come out of Russia in other fields, but second-rate theater, literature, art, etc., are not of great importance in today's international power relationships.

Faced with this formidable and ruthless adversary who has openly promised "to bury" us and who grows daily in industrial and military might, what are we to do?

First, I think, we must awaken America to the danger facing the nation—making public all the facts without soothing the impact of unpleasant truths. I have no doubt that as a people we have enough patriotism, let alone enlightened self-interest, to recognize that we must put greater effort into the things which will make America strong, even if this may require a reappraisal of cherished convictions and ways of life; even at the cost of some material sacrifices, which I doubt would be large.

Ours is an enormously productive economy, the first in history which produces a large surplus over and above reasonable necessities of life. The flood of goods coming off our production lines is so tremendous that some ten billion dollars must be spent annually to encourage disposal of them. I speak, of course, of advertising, which costs us as much as all of our primary and secondary public schools put together. This is money with which advertisers finance our mass media and through them ceaselessly hammer at the need for ever more better goods and services. People must be made to buy things for which they feel no need; they must be induced to replace possessions still entirely satisfactory for new ones which, it is promised, will make them up to date and enhance their family's prestige. The subconscious is probed in order to find ways in which to stifle the still voice of conscience and induce the American people to go into consumer debts of more than three billion dollars annually—42 billion standing on the books as of now. Often young children are conditioned to act as unpaid boosters for higher consumption.

Last year it cost the automobile industry alone 1½ billion dollars to design and bring out new models. This appears to be the only way to insure that American families will continue to spend 10 per cent of their income on cars. One and a half billion dollars is three-fourths of what the nation paid for education in all its public colleges and universities. I mention these figures to show that sacrifices to give America strength in the race with Russia would be insignificant in view of our enormous margin of luxury spending.

Second, and equally important, I believe, we must reverse our treatment of scientists and trained professionals. It is easy to make a good living in this country without much serious education. Hence the temptation to do this is so great that it can be offset only by deliberate actions to elevate the status of professional people in terms both of prestige and of material reward. We had better stop calling scientists "long hairs" or "little men with beards." In the present mood of chastisement, scientists have been speaking up and telling us that such disparaging remarks hurt and may have discouraged many a young man from choosing the hard intellectual road to science rather than the easy and pleasant road to business success and country-club living.

Merely spending a lot of money on scientists, scientific research, and new military projects will not be enough. In final analysis trained man power can only come out of a thoroughly reorganized educational system with totally different aims and considerably higher scholastic standards. To carry through such drastic reforms is a formidable undertaking, but reforms of similar magnitude have been carried out elsewhere in the past.

Much could be learned from Europe's educational experience in particular, for Europe is old and wise at educating the young. Some of her famous universities have been in the business for a longer time than the white man has been in North America. Formal education itself is a European invention, first in colonizing the world and then, so to speak, setting it on its feet with the mark of European civilization so deeply imbedded that it may well prove ineradicable. Nowhere else has there been a spontaneous, native growth; wherever formal education exists today it was brought by European settlers or colonial administrators.

One thing we in this country might learn from Europe is how to keep education in step with changing times. This sometimes necessitates a reform of such magnitude as to resemble a revolution in education. There have been two such upheavals in Russia: in 1917 and in the early 1930's. The first abolished the Czarist school system and established a new type of workers' education, influenced to some degree by the philosophical theories of John Dewey and by American progressive experiments; the second abolished this system and returned to a Marxist version of the continental European system.

There have been other less drastic school reforms elsewhere. In fact the entire nineteenth century was one of constant change toward better and more widespread education in the entire Western world and, influenced by the West, in many underdeveloped countries as well. England changed her education drastically over a period of almost a hundred years, from the mid-1800's until the post-World War II reform period. Once the most aristocratic and expensive education in the world, limited to a small segment of the upper middle class and the aristocracy, English public education is now first-rate in quality and entirely open to all who can qualify. Two other major educational reforms are of interest. One, the reorganization of Prussian education after the country's defeat by Napoleon in 1806; the other France's reorganization of the elementary-school system after her defeat by Prussia in 1871.

No educational reform is ever easy. It is more quickly put through where governments need not consult their people. This gives authoritarian countries such as Prussia an advantage over democratic countries such as England in the matter of keeping education in step with changing conditions. Similarly, it is giving totalitarian Russia an advantage over us which will take great effort on our part to overcome.

*　*　*

In our pride at the number of American children who graduate from high school we forget how few of them have taken an academic course comparable to that of the academic secondary schools in Europe or of the present ten-year school in Russia. Of the 55 per cent who graduate from high schools here, only a very small percentage have learned as much in literature, in their native language, in foreign languages, sciences, mathematics, astronomy, and geography as all of the 39 per cent who graduate from the Russian school. It is evident that our society is such that children are not motivated to obtain a rigorous academic education. It is too easy to make a good living without much of an education. This lack of motivation is dangerous today when the Scientific Revolution is upon us and we need many people with a good liberal-arts background and excellent professional education as well.

I have received many letters from anxious and worried parents. This was gratifying because it gave me hope that something would be done to better our schools. It was not surprising since I expected as much of

American parents. What did surprise me was the interest and concern expressed by foreign correspondents. I should like to quote from a letter written me by a Swiss physician, enclosing a long, carefully thought-out essay on the differences between American and European education; written, I may add, in faultless English! The letter said in part: "In sending you the enclosed, I am fully aware of the fact that America is quite capable of taking care of her problems and of solving them to her own satisfaction. But there are so many of us here who love and admire America and we want her to succeed in her attempt to overtake Russia in science and learning. Be pleased to excuse, if some of us seem to have made a friend's worries our own. We cannot help it. What we fear is Russia's youth with its simple, austere mode of life and the resulting stock pile of time and energy at its disposal for work and study; its rigorous system of education, borrowed from Central Europe, where most of its scientists and educators come from. Yet all of us here want America to lead in scholarship and scientific achievements. *Do you think that dollars alone will do it?*" (My italics.) I often think of these words when I encounter the easy optimism, the blind complacency, the stubborn refusal to take heed of warnings which are characteristic of so many of our progressive educationists. I think of the time and care expended by a friend of America, a citizen of a small sister republic, in order to send me information that might help in my efforts to bring about awareness of the danger in which we find ourselves because of educational deficiencies.

The danger is well understood by all who know about our manpower shortage. At the conclusion of its lengthy investigation into this shortage, the Joint Atomic Energy Committee remarked in a preface to the Hearings on Shortage of Scientific and Engineering Man Power: "The basic issue is whether or not we as a nation are willing to sit by and watch Soviet Russia, with her vast technological training programs, outstrip us in technological development in the coming years, or whether we take action now to see to it that the United States has the trained man power to insure our continued world leadership in this field. We are in a battle for brain power." These are grave words and Sputnik has underlined them for us. As the committee remarks, the testimony before it "is a shocking indictment of America's indifference toward one of the most serious problems facing this nation."

Basically it is an indifference to intellectual excellence, to matters of the mind. We still think more highly of an athlete than of a brilliant student. We still do not as a people realize that in modern life, as White-head said it so elegantly: "The rule is absolute, *the race which does not value trained intelligence is doomed*. Not all your victories on land or at sea can move back the finger of fate. Today we maintain ourselves. Tomorrow science will have moved forward yet one more step, and there will be no appeal from the judgment which will then be pronounced on the uneducated."

BERTRAND RUSSELL

Bertrand Russell was born near Trellock, Wales, on May 18, 1872. After the death of his parents he was brought up by his grandparents in a very Victorian atmosphere. He experienced a number of tutors, and at 18 entered Cambridge University where he studied mathematics and philosophy.

Russell later taught at Cambridge, the University of Chicago, and the University of California. He traveled widely around the world, and became quite a controversial figure for his ideas about marriage, war, and peace. He was a prolific writer, and in 1950 was awarded the Nobel Prize for literature.

Russell wrote a large number of books in a variety of areas. In education his main contributions are *Education and the Social Order, On Education,* and *Education and the Modern World.*

Russell once opened his own school called Beacon Hill where he tried out some of his ideas about educating children. Russell feels that the basic aim of education should be the development of character and intelligence. At Beacon Hill there was an attempt made to instill courage, independence, and a sense of self-discipline in the child, which Russell feels should be the aims of any good educational program.

Russell feels that we need to turn out more persons who do not acquiesce to dogma and scepticism, but rather, are people with an unquenchable thirst for knowledge. He believes that the schools should develop more individualism while at the same time encouraging people to love their fellow human beings.

EDUCATION AND THE GOOD LIFE

Bertrand Russell

The American public schools achieve successfully a task never before attempted on a large scale: the task of transforming a heterogeneous selection of mankind into a homogeneous nation. This is done so ably, and is on the whole such a beneficent work, that on the balance great praise is due to those who accomplish it. But America, like Japan, is placed in a peculiar situation, and what the special circumstances justify is not necessarily an ideal to be followed everywhere and always. America has had certain advantages and certain difficulties. Among the advantages were: a higher standard of wealth; freedom from the danger of defeat in war; comparative absence of cramping traditions inherited from the Middle Ages. Immigrants found in America a generally diffused sentiment of democracy and an advanced stage of industrial technique. These, I think, are the two chief reasons why almost all of them came to admire America more than their native countries. But actual immigrants, as a rule, retain a dual patriotism: in European struggles they continue to take passionately the side of the nation to which they originally belonged. Their children, on the contrary, lose all loyalty to the country from which their parents have come, and become merely and simply Americans. The attitude of the parents is attributable to the general merits of America; that of the children is very largely determined by their school education. It is only the contribution of the school that concerns us.

In so far as the school can rely upon the genuine merits of America, there is no need to associate the teaching of American patriotism with

---

Bertrand Russell, *Education and the Good Life*, Boni and Liveright, New York, 1926, pp. 55-61, 82-83, 314-319.

the inculcation of false standards. But where the Old World is superior to the New, it becomes necessary to instill a contempt for genuine excellences. The intellectual level in Western Europe and the artistic level in Eastern Europe are, on the whole, higher than in America. Throughout Western Europe, except in Spain and Portugal, there is less theological superstition than in America. In almost all European countries the individual is less subject to herd domination than in America: his inner freedom is greater even where his political freedom is less. In these respects, the American public schools do harm. The harm is essential to the teaching of an exclusive American patriotism. The harm, as with the Japanese and the Jesuits, comes from regarding the pupils as means to an end, not as ends in themselves. The teacher should love his children better than his State or his Church; otherwise he is not an ideal teacher.

When I say that pupils should be regarded as ends, not as means, I may be met by the retort that, after all, everybody is more important as a means than as an end. What a man is as an end perishes when he dies; what he produces as a means continues to the end of time. We cannot deny this, but we can deny the consequences deducted from it. A man's importance as a means may be for good or for evil; the remote effects of human actions are so uncertain that a wise man will tend to dismiss them from his calculations. Broadly speaking, good men have good effects, and bad men bad effects. This, of course, is not an invariable law of nature. A bad man may murder a tyrant because he has committed crimes which the tyrant intends to punish; the effects of his act may be good, though he and his act are bad. Nevertheless, as a broad general rule, a community of men and women who are intrinsically excellent will have better effects than one composed of people who are ignorant and malevolent. Apart from such considerations, children and young people feel instinctively the difference between those who genuinely wish them well and those who regard them merely as raw material for some scheme. Neither character nor intelligence will develop as well or as freely where the teacher is deficient in love; and love of this kind consists essentially in *feeling* the child as an end. We all have this feeling about ourselves: we desire good things for ourselves without first demanding a proof that some great purpose will be furthered by our obtaining them. Every ordinarily affectionate parent feels the same sort of thing about his or her children. Parents want their children to grow, to be strong and healthy, to do well at school, and so on, in just the same way in which they want things for themselves; no effort of self-denial and no abstract principle of justice is involved in taking trouble about such matters. This parental instinct is not always strictly confined to one's own children. In its diffused form, it must exist in anyone who is to be a good teacher of little boys and girls. As the pupils grow older, it grows less important. But only those who possess it can be trusted to draw up schemes of education. Those who regard it as one of the purposes of male education to produce men willing to kill and be killed for frivolous reasons are clearly deficient in diffused parental feeling; yet they control education in all civilized countries except Denmark and China.

But it is not enough that the educator should love the young; it is necessary also that he should have a right conception of human excellence. Cats teach their kittens to catch mice and play with them; militarists do likewise with the human young. The cat loves the kitten, but not the mouse; the militarist may love his own son, but not the sons of his country's enemies. Even those who love all mankind may err through a wrong conception of the good life. I shall try, therefore, before going any further, to give an idea of what I consider excellent in men and women, quite without regard to practicality, or to the educational methods by which it might be brought into being. Such a picture will help us afterwards, when we come to consider the details of education; we shall know the direction in which we wish to move.

We must first make a distinction: some qualities are desirable in a certain proportion of mankind, others are desirable universally. We want artists, but we also want men of science. We want great administrators, but we also want ploughmen and millers and bakers. The qualities which produce a man of great eminence in some one direction are often such as might be undesirable if they were universal. Shelley describes the day's work of a poet as follows:

> He will watch from dawn to floom
> The lake-reflected sun illume
> The honey-bees in the ivy bloom,
> Nor heed nor see what things they be.

These habits are praiseworthy in a poet, but not—shall we say—in a postman. We cannot therefore frame our education with a view to giving every one the temperament of a poet. But some characteristics are universally desirable, and it is these alone that I shall consider at this stage.

189

I make no distinction between male and female excellence. A certain amount of occupational training is desirable for a woman who is to have the care of babies, but that only involves the same sort of difference as there is between a farmer and a miller. It is in no degree fundamental, and does not demand consideration at our present level.

I will take four characteristics which seem to me jointly to form the basis for an ideal character: vitality, courage, sensitiveness, and intelligence. I do not suggest that this list is complete, but I think it carries us a good way. Moreover, I firmly believe that, by proper physical, emotional and intellectual care of the young, these qualities could all be made very common.

* * *

A community of men and women possessing vitality, courage, sensitiveness, and intelligence, in the highest degree that education can produce, would be very different from anything that has hitherto existed. Very few people would be unhappy. The main causes of unhappiness at present are: ill-health, poverty, and an unsatisfactory sex-life. All of these would become very rare. Good health could be almost universal, and even old age could be postponed. Poverty, since the industrial revolution, is only due to collective stupidity. Sensitiveness would make people wish to abolish it, intelligence would show them the way, and courage would lead them to adopt it. (A timid person would rather remain miserable than do anything unusual.) Most people's sex-life, at present, is more or less unsatisfactory. This is partly due to bad education, partly to persecution by the authorities and Mrs. Grundy. A generation of women brought up without irrational sex fears would soon make an end of this. Fear has been thought the only way to make women "virtuous," and they have been deliberately taught to be cowards, both physically and mentally. Women in whom love is cramped encourage brutality and hypocrisy in their husbands, and distort the instincts of their children. One generation of fearless women could transform the world, by bringing into it a generation of fearless children, not contorted into unnatural shapes, but straight and candid, generous, affectionate, and free. Their ardor would sweep away the cruelty and pain which we endure because we are lazy, cowardly, hardhearted and stupid. It is education that gives us these bad qualities, and education that must give us the opposite virtues. Education is the key to the new world.

* * *

Knowledge wielded by love is what the educator needs and what his pupils should acquire. In earlier years, love towards the pupils is the most important kind; in later years, love of the knowledge imparted becomes increasingly necessary. The important knowledge at first is knowledge of physiology, hygiene, and psychology, of which the last more especially concerns the teacher. The instincts and reflexes with which a child is born can be developed by the environment into the most diverse habits, and therefore into the most diverse characters. Most of this happens in very early childhood; consequently it is at this period that we can most hopefully attempt to form character. Those who like existing evils are fond of asserting that human nature cannot be changed. If they mean that it cannot be changed after six years old, there is a measure of truth in what they say. If they mean that nothing can be done to alter the instincts and reflexes with which an infant is born, they are again more or less in the right, though of course eugenics could, and perhaps will, produce remarkable results even here. But if they mean, as they usually do, that there is no way of producing an adult population whose behavior will be radically different from that of existing populations, they are flying in the fact of all modern psychology. Given two infants with the same character at birth, different early environments may turn them into adults with totally different dispositions. It is the business of early education to train the instincts so that they may produce a harmonious character, constructive rather than destructive, affectionate rather than sullen, courageous, frank, and intelligent. All this can be done with a great majority of children; it is actually being done where children are rightly treated. If existing knowledge were used and tested methods applied, we could, in a generation, produce a population almost wholly free from disease, malevolence, and stupidity. We do not do so, because we prefer oppression and war.

The crude material of instinct is, in most respects, equally capable of leading to desirable and to undesirable actions. In the past, men did not understand the training of instinct, and therefore were compelled to resort to repression. Punishment and fear were the great incentives to what was called virtue. We now know that repression is a bad method, both because it is never really successful, and because it produces mental disorders. The training of instincts is a totally different method, involving a totally different technique. Habits and skill make, as it were, a channel for instinct, leading it to flow one way or another according to

191

the direction of the channel. By creating the right habits and the right skill, we cause the child's instincts themselves to prompt desirable actions. There is no sense of strain, because there is no need to resist temptation. There is no thwarting, and the child has a sense of unfettered spontaneity. I do not mean these statements to be taken in an absolute sense; there will always be unforeseen contingencies in which older methods may become necessary. But the more the science of child psychology is perfected, and the more experience we acquire in nursery-schools, the more perfectly the new methods can be applied.

I have tried to bring before the reader the wonderful possibilities which are now open to us. Think what it would mean: health, freedom, happiness, kindness, intelligence, all nearly universal. In one generation, if we chose, we could bring the millennium.

But none of this can come about without love. The knowledge exists; lack of love prevents it from being applied. Sometimes the lack of love towards children brings me near to despair—for example, when I find almost all our recognized moral leaders unwilling that anything should be done to prevent the birth of children with venereal disease. Nevertheless, there is a gradual liberation of love of children, which surely is one of our natural impulses. Ages of fierceness have overlaid what is naturally kindly in the dispositions of ordinary men and women. It is only lately that many Christians have ceased the damnation of unbaptized infants. Nationalism is another doctrine which dries up the springs of humanity; during the war, we caused almost all German children to suffer from rickets. We must let loose our natural kindliness; if a doctrine demands that we should inflict misery upon children, let us reject it, however dear it may be to us. In almost all cases, the psychological source of cruel doctrines is fear; that is one reason why I have laid so much stress upon the elimination of fear in childhood. Let us root out the fears that lurk in the dark places of our own minds. The possibilities of a happy world that are opened up by modern education make it well worth while to run some personal risk, even if the risk were more real than it is.

When we have created young people freed from fear and inhibitions and rebellious or thwarted instincts, we shall be able to open to them the world of knowledge, freely and completely, without dark hidden corners; and if instruction is wisely given, it will be a joy rather than a task to those who receive it. It is not important to increase the amount of what is learnt above that now usually taught to the children of the professional classes. What is important is the spirit of adventure and liberty, the sense of setting out upon a voyage of discovery. If formal education is given in this spirit, all the more intelligent pupils will supplement it by their own efforts, for which every opportunity should be provided. Knowledge is the liberator from the empire of natural forces and destructive passions; without knowledge, the world of our hopes cannot be built. A generation educated in fearless freedom will have wider and bolder hopes than are possible to us, who still have to struggle with the superstitious fears that lie in wait for us below the level of consciousness. Not we, but the free men and women whom we shall create, must see the new world, first in their hopes, and then at last in the full splendor of reality.

The way is clear. Do we love our children enough to take it? Or shall we let them suffer as we have suffered? Shall we let them be twisted and stunted and terrified in youth, to be killed afterwards in futile wars which their intelligence was too cowed to prevent? A thousand ancient fears obstruct the road to happiness and freedom. But love can conquer fear, and if we love our children nothing can make us withhold the great gift which it is in our power to bestow.

B. F. SKINNER

B. F. Skinner was born in Susquehanna, Pennsylvania, on March 20, 1904. He graduated from Susquehanna High School in 1922 and then attended Hamilton College in Clinton, New York, where he majored in English literature. He went to Harvard where he received an M.A. degree in psychology in 1930 and his Ph.D. degree in 1931. From 1931 to 1933 he worked under a fellowship from the National Research Council, and from 1933 to 1936 he was a junior fellow of the Harvard Society of Fellows. He taught at the University of Minnesota and at the University of Indiana, and then returned in 1947 to serve on the faculty at Harvard. In 1958 he became the Edgar Pierce Professor of Psychology at Harvard.

Skinner has written a number of books dealing with psychology and education such as *The Behavior of Organisms, Verbal Behavior, Cumulative Record, Schedules of Reinforcement, Science and Human Behavior,* and *Walden Two.*

Skinner is very much associated with conditioning and programmed instruction, and is considered to be the father of the teaching machine. Skinner believes that contemporary education does not make enough use of the discoveries of science, particularly that of operant conditioning. Positive reinforcement or immediate reward, he feels, are greatly lacking in classrooms, and Skinner advocates more forms of conditioning in the classroom. He feels that we cannot hope to improve education by only building more schools and training more teachers. What we really need, he believes, is a revision in our curriculum and methods of teaching as well.

THE SCIENCE OF LEARNING AND
THE ART OF TEACHING

B. F. Skinner

Some promising advances have recently been made in the field of learning. Special techniques have been designed to arrange what are called "contingencies of reinforcement"—the relations which prevail between behavior on the one hand and the consequences of that behavior on the other—with the result that a much more effective control of behavior has been achieved. It has long been argued that an organism learns mainly by producing changes in its environment, but it is only recently that these changes have been carefully manipulated. In traditional devices for the study of learning—in the serial maze, for example, or in the T-maze, the problem box, or the familiar discrimination apparatus—the effects produced by the organism's behavior are left to many fluctuating circumstances. There is many a slip between the turn-to-the-right and the food-cup at the end of the alley. It is not surprising that techniques of this sort have yielded only very rough data from which the uniformities demanded by an experimental science can be extracted only by averaging many cases. In none of this work has the behavior of the individual organism been predicted in more than a statistical sense. The learning processes which are the presumed object of such research are reached only through a series of inferences. Current preoccupation with deductive systems reflects this state of the science.

Recent improvements in the conditions which control behavior in the field of learning are of two principal sorts. The Law of Effect has

B. F. Skinner, "The Science of Learning and the Art of Teaching," *Harvard Educational Review*, 24, Spring 1954, 86-87, 89-97. Copyright © 1954 by President and Fellows of Harvard College.

been taken seriously; we have made sure that effects *do* occur and that they occur under conditions which are optimal for producing the changes called learning. Once we have arranged the particular type of consequence called a reinforcement, our techniques permit us to shape up the behavior of an organism almost at will. It has become a routine exercise to demonstrate this in classes in elementary psychology by conditioning such an organism as a pigeon. Simply by presenting food to a hungry pigeon at the right time, it is possible to shape up three or four well-defined responses in a single demonstration period—such responses as turning around, pacing the floor in the pattern of a figure-8, standing still in a corner of the demonstration apparatus, stretching the neck, or stamping the foot. Extremely complex performances may be reached through successive stages in the shaping process, the contingencies of reinforcement being changed progressively in the direction of the required behavior. The results are often quite dramatic. In such a demonstration one can *see* learning take place. A significant change in behavior is often obvious as the result of a single reinforcement.

* * *

One of the most dramatic applications of these techniques has recently been made in the Harvard Psychological Laboratories by Floyd Ratliff and Donald S. Blough, who have skillfully used multiple and serial schedules of reinforcement to study complex perceptual processes in the infrahuman organism. They have achieved a sort of psycho-physics without verbal instruction. In a recent experiment by Blough, for example, a pigeon draws a detailed dark-adaptation curve showing the characteristic breaks of rod and cone vision. The curve is recorded continuously in a single experimental period and is quite comparable with the curves of human subjects. The pigeon behaves in a way which, in the human case, we would not hesitate to describe by saying that it adjusts a very faint patch of light until it can just be seen.

In all this work, the species of the organism has made surprisingly little difference. It is true that the organisms studied have all been vertebrates, but they still cover a wide range. Comparable results have been obtained with pigeons, rats, dogs, monkeys, human children, and most recently, by the author in collaboration with Ogden R. Lindsley, human psychotic subjects. In spite of great phylogenetic differences, all these organisms show amazingly similar properties of the learning process.

It should be emphasized that this has been achieved by analyzing the effects of reinforcement and by designing techniques which manipulate reinforcement with considerable precision. Only in this way can the behavior of the individual organism be brought under such precise control. It is also important to note that through a gradual advance to complex interrelations among responses, the same degree of rigor is being extended to behavior which would usually be assigned to such fields as perception, thinking, and personality dynamics.

From this exciting prospect of an advancing science of learning, it is a great shock to turn to that branch of technology which is most directly concerned with the learning process—education. Let us consider, for example, the teaching of arithmetic in the lower grades. The school is concerned with imparting to the child a large number of responses of a special sort. The responses are all verbal. They consist of speaking and writing certain words, figures, and signs which, to put it roughly, refer to numbers and to arithmetic operations. The first task is to shape up these responses—to get the child to pronounce and to write responses correctly, but the principal task is to bring this behavior under many sorts of stimulus control. This is what happens when the child learns to count, to recite tables, to count while ticking off the items in an assemblage of objects, to respond to spoken or written numbers by saying "odd," "even," "prime," and so on. Over and above this elaborate repertoire of numerical behavior, most of which is often dismissed as the product of rote learning, the teaching of arithmetic looks forward to those complex serial arrangements of responses involved in original mathematical thinking. The child must acquire responses of transposing, clearing fractions, and so on, which modify the order or pattern of the original material so that the response called a solution is eventually made possible.

Now, how is this extremely complicated verbal repertoire set up? In the first place, what reinforcements are used? Fifty years ago the answer would have been clear. At that time educational control was still frankly aversive. The child read numbers, copied numbers, memorized tables, and performed operations upon numbers to escape the threat of the birch rod or cane. Some positive reinforcements were perhaps eventually derived from the increased efficiency of the child in the field of arithmetic and in rare cases some automatic reinforcements may have resulted from the sheer manipulation of the medium—from the solution of problems or the discovery of the intricacies of the number system. But for the immediate purposes of education the child acted to avoid or escape punishment. It was part of the reform movement known as progressive education to make the positive consequences more immediately effective, but any one who visits the lower grades of the average school today will observe that a change has been made, not from aversive to positive control, but from one form of aversive stimulation to another. The child at his desk, filling in his workbook, is behaving primarily to escape from the threat of a series of minor aversive events—the teacher's displeasure, the criticism or ridicule of his classmates, an ignominious showing in a competition, low marks, a trip to the office "to be talked to" by the principal, or a word to the parent who may still resort to the birch rod. In this welter of aversive consequences, getting the right answer is in itself an insignificant event, any effect of which is lost amid the anxieties, the boredom, and the aggressions which are the inevitable by-products of aversive control.

Secondly, we have to ask how the contingencies of reinforcement are arranged. When is a numerical operation reinforced as "right"? Eventually, of course, the pupil may be able to check his own answers and achieve some sort of automatic reinforcement, but in the early stages the reinforcement of being right is usually accorded by the teacher. The contingencies she provides are far from optimal. It can easily be demonstrated that, unless explicit mediating behavior has been set up, the lapse of only a few seconds between response and reinforcement destroys most of the effect. In a typical classroom, nevertheless, long periods of time customarily elapse. The teacher may walk up and down the aisle, for example, while the class is working on a sheet of problems, pausing here and there to say right or wrong. Many seconds or minutes intervene between the child's response and the teacher's reinforcement. In many cases—for example, when papers are taken home to be corrected—as much as 24 hours may intervene. It is surprising that this system has any effect whatsoever.

A third notable shortcoming is the lack of a skillful program which moves forward through a series of progressive approximations to the final complex behavior desired. A long series of contingencies is necessary to bring the organism into the possession of mathematical behavior most efficiently. But the teacher is seldom able to reinforce at each step in such a series because she cannot deal with the pupil's responses one at a time. It is usually necessary to reinforce the behavior in blocks of responses—as in correcting a work sheet or page from a workbook. The responses within such a block must not be interrelated. The answer to one problem must not depend upon the answer to another. The number of stages through which one may progressively approach a complex pattern of behavior is therefore small, and the task so much the more difficult. Even the most modern workbook in beginning arithmetic is far from exemplifying an efficient program for shaping up mathematical behavior.

Perhaps the most serious criticism of the current classroom is the relative infrequency of reinforcement. Since the pupil is usually dependent upon the teacher for being right, and since many pupils are usually dependent upon the same teacher, the total number of contingencies which may be arranged during, say, the first four years, is of the order of only a few thousand. But a very rough estimate suggests that efficient mathematical behavior at this level requires something of the order of 25,000 contingencies. We may suppose that even in the brighter student a given contingency must be arranged several times to place the behavior well in hand. The responses to be set up are not simply the various items in tables of addition, subtraction, multiplication, and division; we have also to consider the alternative forms in which each item may be stated. To the learning of such material we should add hundreds of responses concerned with factoring, identifying primes, memorizing series, using short-cut techniques of calculation, constructing and using geometric representations or number forms, and so on. Over and above all this, the whole mathematical repertoire must be brought under the control of concrete problems of considerable variety. Perhaps 50,000 contingencies is a more conservative estimate. In their frame of reference the daily assignment in arithmetic seems pitifully meager.

The result of all this is, of course, well known. Even our best schools are under criticism for their inefficiency in the teaching of drill subjects such as arithmetic. The condition in the average school is a matter of widespread national concern. Modern children simply do not learn arithmetic quickly or well. Nor is the result simply incompetence. The very subjects in which modern techniques are weakest are those in which failure is most conspicuous, and in the wake of an ever-growing incompetence come the anxieties, uncertainties, and aggressions which in their turn present other problems to the school. Most pupils soon claim the asylum of not being "ready" for arithmetic at a given level or, eventually, of not having a mathematical mind. Such explanations are readily seized upon by defensive teachers and parents. Few pupils ever reach the stage at which automatic reinforcements follow as the natural consequences of mathematical behavior. On the contrary, the figures and symbols of mathematics have become standard emotional stimuli. The glimpse of a column of figures, not to say an algebraic symbol or an integral sign, is likely to set off—not mathematical behavior—but a reaction of anxiety, guilt, or fear.

The teacher is usually no happier about this than the pupil. Denied the opportunity to control via the birch rod, quite at sea as to the mode of operation of the few techniques at her disposal, she spends as little time as possible on drill subjects and eagerly subscribes to philosophies of education which emphasize material of greater inherent interest. A confession of weakness is her extraordinary concern lest the child be taught something unnecessary. The repertoire to be imparted is carefully reduced to an essential minimum. In the field of spelling, for example, a great deal of time and energy has gone into discovering just those words which the young child is going to use, as if it were a crime to waste one's educational power in teaching an unnecessary word. Eventually, weakness of technique emerges in the disguise of a reformulation of the aims of education. Skills are minimized in favor of vague achievements—educating for democracy, educating the whole child, educating for life, and so on. And there the matter ends; for, unfortunately, these philosophies do not in turn suggest improvements in techniques. They offer little or no help in the design of better classroom practices.

There would be no point in urging these objections if improvement were impossible. But the advances which have recently been made in our control of the learning process suggest a thorough revision of classroom practices and, fortunately, they tell us how the revision can be brought about. This is not, of course, the first time that the results of an experimental science have been brought to bear upon the practical problems of education. The modern classroom does not, however, offer much evidence that research in the field of learning has been respected or used. This condition is no doubt partly due to the limitations of earlier research. But it has been encouraged by a too hasty conclusion that the laboratory study of learning is inherently limited because it cannot take into account the realities of the classroom. In the light of our increasing knowledge of the learning process we should, instead, insist upon dealing with those realities and forcing a substantial change in them. Education is perhaps the most important branch of scientific technology. It deeply affects the lives of all of us. We can no longer allow the exigencies of a practical situation to suppress the tremendous improvements which are within reach. The practical situation must be changed.

There are certain questions which have to be answered in turning to the study of any new organism. What behavior is to be set up? What reinforcers are at hand? What responses are available in embarking upon a program of progressive approximation which will lead to the final form of the behavior? How can reinforcements be most efficiently scheduled to maintain the behavior in strength? These questions are all relevant in considering the problem of the child in the lower grades.

In the first place, what reinforcements are available? What does the school have in its possession which will reinforce a child? We may look first to the material to be learned, for it is possible that this will provide considerable automatic reinforcement. Children play for hours with mechanical toys, paints, scissors and paper, noise-makers, puzzles—in short, with almost anything which feeds back significant changes in the environment and is reasonably free of aversive properties. The sheer control of nature is itself reinforcing. This effect is not evident in the modern school because it is masked by the emotional responses generated by aversive control. It is true that automatic reinforcement from the manipulation of the environment is probably only a mild reinforcer and may need to be carefully husbanded, but one of the most striking principles to emerge from recent research is that the *net* amount of reinforcement is of little significance. A very slight reinforcement may be tremendously effective in controlling behavior if it is wisely used.

If the natural reinforcement inherent in the subject matter is not enough, other reinforcers must be employed. Even in school the child is occasionally permitted to do "what he wants to do," and access to reinforcements of many sorts may be made contingent upon the more immediate consequences of the behavior to be established. Those who advocate competition as a useful social motive may wish to use the reinforcements which follow from excelling others, although there is the difficulty that in this case the reinforcement of one child is necessarily aversive to another. Next in order we might place the good will and affection of the teacher, and only when that has failed need we turn to the use of aversive stimulation.

In the second place, how are these reinforcements to be made contingent upon the desired behavior? There are two considerations here—the gradual elaboration of extremely complex patterns of behavior and the maintenance of the behavior in strength at each stage. The whole process of becoming competent in any field must be divided into a very large number of very small steps, and reinforcement must be contingent upon the accomplishment of each step. This solution to the problem of creating a complex repertoire of behavior also solves the problem of maintaining the behavior in strength. We could, of course, resort to the techniques of scheduling already developed in the study of other organisms but in the present state of our knowledge of educational practices, scheduling appears to be most effectively arranged through the design of the material to be learned. By making each successive step as small as possible, the frequency of reinforcement can be raised to a maximum, while the possibly aversive consequences of being wrong are reduced to a minimum. Other ways of designing material would yield other programs of reinforcement. Any supplementary reinforcement would probably have to be scheduled in the more traditional way.

These requirements are not excessive, but they are probably incompatible with the current realities of the classroom. In the experimental study of learning it has been found that the contingencies of reinforcement which are most efficient in controlling the organism cannot be arranged through the personal mediation of the experimenter. An organism is affected by subtle details of contingencies which are beyond the capacity of the human organism to arrange. Mechanical and electrical devices must be used. Mechanical help is also demanded by the sheer number of contingencies which may be used efficiently in a single experimental session. We have recorded many millions of responses from a single organism during thousands of experimental hours. Personal arrangement of the contingencies and personal observation of the results are quite unthinkable. Now, the human organism is, if anything, more sensitive to precise contingencies than the other organisms we have studied. We have every reason to expect, therefore, that the most effective control of human learning will require instrumental aid. The simple fact is that, as a mere reinforcing mechanism, the teacher is out of date. This would be true even if a single teacher devoted all her time to a single child, but her inadequacy is multiplied many-fold when she must serve as a reinforcing device to many children at once. If the teacher is to take advantage of recent advances in the study of learning, she must have the help of mechanical devices.

The technical problem of providing the necessary instrumental aid is not particularly difficult. There are many ways in which the necessary contingencies may be arranged, either mechanically or electrically. An inexpensive device which solves most of the principal problems has already been constructed. It is still in the experimental stage, but a description will suggest the kind of instrument which seems to be required. The device consists of a small box about the size of a small record player. On the top surface is a window through which a question or problem printed on a paper tape may be seen. The child answers the question by moving one or more sliders upon which the digits 0 through 9 are printed. The answer appears in square holes punched in the paper upon which the question is printed. When the answer has been set, the child turns a knob. The operation is as simple as adjusting a television set. If the answer is right, the knob turns freely and can be made to ring a bell or provide some other conditioned reinforcement. If the answer is wrong, the knob will not turn. A counter may be added to tally wrong answers. The knob must then be reversed slightly and a second attempt at a right answer made. (Unlike the flash-card, the device reports a wrong answer without giving the right answer.) When the answer is right, a further turn of the knob engages a clutch which moves the next problem into place in the window. This movement cannot be completed, however, until the sliders have been returned to zero.

The important features of the device are these: Reinforcement for the right answer is immediate. The mere manipulation of the device will probably be reinforcing enough to keep the average pupil at work for a suitable period each day, provided traces of earlier aversive control can be wiped out. A teacher may supervise an entire class at work on such devices at the same time, yet each child may progress at his own rate, completing as many problems as possible within the class period. If forced to be away from school, he may return to pick up where he left off. The gifted child will advance rapidly, but can be kept from getting too far ahead either by being excused from arithmetic for a time or by being given special sets of problems which take him into some of the interesting bypaths of mathematics.

The device makes it possible to present carefully designed material in which one problem can depend upon the answer to the preceding and where, therefore, the most efficient progress to an eventually complex repertoire can be made. Provision has been made for recording the commonest mistakes so that the tapes can be modified as experience dictates. Additional steps can be inserted where pupils tend to have trouble, and ultimately the material will reach a point at which the answers of the average child will almost always be right.

If the material itself proves not to be sufficiently reinforcing, other reinforcers in the possession of the teacher or school may be made contingent upon the operation of the device or upon progress through a series of problems. Supplemental reinforcement would not sacrifice the advantages gained from immediate reinforcement and from the possibility of constructing an optimal series of steps which approach the complex repertoire of mathematical behavior most efficiently.

A similar device in which the sliders carry the letters of the alphabet has been designed to teach spelling. In addition to the advantages which can be gained from precise reinforcement and careful programming, the device will teach reading at the same time. It can also be used to establish the large and important repertoire of verbal relationships encountered in logic and science. In short, it can teach verbal thinking. As to content instruction, the device can be operated as a multiple-choice self-rater.

Some objections to the use of such devices in the classroom can easily be foreseen. The cry will be raised that the child is being treated as a mere animal and that an essentially human intellectual achievement is being analyzed in unduly mechanistic terms. Mathematical behavior is usually regarded, not as a repertoire of responses involving numbers and numerical operations, but as evidences of mathematical ability or the exercise of the power of reason. It is true that the techniques which are emerging from the experimental study of learning are not designed to "develop the mind" or to further some vague "understanding" of mathematical relationships. They are designed, on the contrary, to establish the very behaviors which are taken to be the evidences of such mental states or processes. This is only a special case of the general change which is under way in the interpretation of human affairs. An advancing science continues to offer more and more convincing alternatives to traditional formulations. The behavior in terms of which human thinking must eventually be defined is worth treating in its own right as the substantial goal of education.

Of course the teacher has a more important function than to say right or wrong. The changes proposed would free her for the effective exercise of that function. Marking a set of papers in arithmetic—"Yes, nine and six *are* fifteen; no, nine and seven *are not* eighteen"—is beneath the dignity of any intelligent individual. There is more important work to be done—in which the teacher's relations to the pupil cannot be duplicated by a mechanical device. Instrumental help would merely improve these relations. One might say that the main trouble with education in the lower grades today is that the child is obviously not competent and *knows it* and that the teacher is unable to do anything about it and *knows that too*. If the advances which have recently been made in our control of behavior can give the child a genuine competence in reading, writing, spelling, and arithmetic, then the teacher may begin to function, not in lieu of a cheap machine, but through intellectual, cultural, and emotional contacts of that distinctive sort which testify to her status as a human being.

Another possible objection is that mechanized instruction will mean technological unemployment. We need not worry about this until there are enough teachers to go around and until the hours and energy demanded of the teacher are comparable to those in other fields of employment. Mechanical devices will eliminate the more tiresome labors of the teacher but they will not necessarily shorten the time during which she remains in contact with the pupil.

A more practical objection: Can we afford to mechanize our schools? The answer is clearly yes. The device I have just described could be produced as cheaply as a small radio or phonograph. There would need to be far fewer devices than pupils, for they could be used in rotation. But even if we suppose that the instrument eventually found to be most effective would cost several hundred dollars and that large numbers of them would be required, our economy should be able to stand the strain. Once we have accepted the possibility and the necessity of mechanical help in the classroom, the economic problem can easily be surmounted. There is no reason why the school room should be any less mechanized than, for example, the kitchen. A country which annually produces millions of refrigerators, dish-washers, automatic washing machines, automatic clothes-driers, and automatic garbage disposers can certainly afford the equipment necessary to educate its citizens to high standards of competence in the most effective way.

There is a simple job to be done. The task can be stated in concrete terms. The necessary techniques are known. The equipment needed can easily be provided. Nothing stands in the way but cultural inertia. But what is more characteristic of America than an unwillingness to accept the traditional as inevitable? We are on the threshold of an exciting and revolutionary period, in which the scientific study of man will be put to work in man's best interests. Education must play its part. It must accept the fact that a sweeping revision of educational practices is possible and inevitable. When it has done this, we may look forward with confidence to a school system which is aware of the nature of its tasks, secure in its methods, and generously supported by the informed and effective citizens whom education itself will create.

ALFRED NORTH WHITEHEAD

Alfred North Whitehead was born at Ramsgate, Isle of Thanet, Kent, England, on February 15, 1861. He underwent the traditional education of the time with Latin at 10 and Greek at 12. His leisure time interests were history and poetry, particularly the poetry of Wordsworth and Shelley.

At 19 Whitehead entered Trinity College in Cambridge to study mathematics. After completing his studies at Cambridge he became a teacher of mathematics, teaching at both the University of London and at the Imperial College of Science and Technology at Kensington. Whitehead has also been an ardent student of philosophy, and in 1924, at the age of 63, he joined the faculty of Harvard University as professor of philosophy, where he remained until 1937. In 1931 he was made a Fellow of the British Academy and in 1945 was awarded the British Order of Merit. He died in Cambridge, Massachusetts, on December 30, 1947.

Whitehead has written a number of books on philosophy, mathematics, and education, and his *Aims of Education* has been heralded as an important and popular book. The *Aims of Education* was developed from addresses which Whitehead gave to educational groups and scientific societies. Primarily, the intent of the book is to prod teachers into getting rid of dead knowledge or "inert" ideas, i.e., knowledge and ideas that are merely received into the mind without being utilized, tested, or thrown into fresh combinations. He feels that at the present time our schools are overladen with inert ideas, making education both useless and harmful. Whitehead has also been strongly critical of what he feels is overspecialization, and believes that we need to adopt a "metaphysical" attitude toward education which will insure that we deal with significant questions, and deal with knowledge in a unified way.

THE AIMS OF EDUCATION

Alfred North Whitehead

In the history of education, the most striking phenomenon is that schools of learning, which at one epoch are alive with a ferment of genius, in a succeeding generation exhibit merely pedantry and routine. The reason is, that they are overladen with inert ideas. Education with inert ideas is not only useless: it is, above all things, harmful—*Corruptio optimi, pessima.* Except at rare intervals of intellectual ferment, education in the past has been radically infected with inert ideas. That is the reason why uneducated clever women, who have seen much of the world, are in middle life so much the most cultured part of the community. They have been saved from this horrible burden of inert ideas. Every intellectual revolution which has ever stirred humanity into greatness has been a passionate protest against inert ideas. Then, alas, with pathetic ignorance of human psychology, it has proceeded by some educational scheme to bind humanity afresh with inert ideas of its own fashioning.

Let us now ask how in our system of education we are to guard against this mental dryrot. We enunciate two educational commandments. "Do not teach too many subjects," and again, "What you teach, teach thoroughly."

The result of teaching small parts of a large number of subjects is the passive reception of disconnected ideas, not illumined with any spark of vitality. Let the main ideas which are introduced into a child's education be few and important, and let them be thrown into every combination possible. The child should make them his own, and should understand their application here and now in the circumstances of his actual life. From the very beginning of his education, the child should experience the joy of discovery. The discovery which he has to make, is that general ideas give an understanding of that stream of events which pours through his life, which is his life. By understanding I mean more than a mere logical analysis, though that is included. I mean "understanding" in the sense in which it is used in the French proverb, "To understand all, is to forgive all." Pedants sneer at an education which is useful. But if education is not useful, what is it? Is it a talent, to be hidden away in a napkin? Of course, education should be useful, whatever your aim in life. It was useful to Saint Augustine and it was useful to Napoleon. It is useful, because understanding is useful.

I pass lightly over that understanding which should be given by the literary side of education. Nor do I wish to be supposed to pronounce on the relative merits of a classical or a modern curriculum. I would only remark that the understanding which we want is an understanding of an insistent present. The only use of a knowledge of the past is to equip us for the present. No more deadly harm can be done to young minds than by depreciation of the present. The present contains all that there is. It is holy ground; for it is the past, and it is the future. At the same time it must be observed that an age is no less past if it existed two hundred years ago than if it existed two thousand years ago. Do not be deceived by the pedantry of dates. The ages of Shakespeare and of Molière are no less past than are the ages of Sophocles and of Virgil. The communion of saints is a great and inspiring assemblage, but it has only one possible hall of meeting, and that is, the present; and the mere lapse of time through which any particular group of saints must travel to reach that meeting-place, makes very little difference.

Passing now to the scientific and logical side of education, we remember that here also ideas which are not utilized are positively harmful. By utilizing an idea, I mean relating it to that stream, compounded of sense perceptions, feelings, hopes, desires, and of mental activities adjusting thought to thought, which forms our life. I can imagine a set of beings which might fortify their souls by passively reviewing disconnected ideas. Humanity is not built that way—except perhaps some editors of newspapers.

In scientific training, the first thing to do with an idea is to prove it. But allow me for one moment to extend the meaning of "prove"; I mean—to prove its worth. Now an idea is not worth much unless the propositions in which it is embodied are true. Accordingly an essential part of the proof of an idea is the proof, either by experiment or by logic, of the truth of the propositions. But it is not essential that this proof of the truth should constitute the first introduction to the idea. After all, its assertion by the authority of respectable teachers is sufficient evidence to begin with. In our first contact with a set of propositions, we commence by appreciating their importance. That is what we all do in after-life. We do not attempt, in the strict sense, to prove or to disprove anything, unless its importance makes it worthy of that honor. These two processes of proof, in the narrow sense, and of appreciation, do not require a rigid separation in time. Both can be proceeded with nearly concurrently. But in so far as either process must have the priority, it should be that of appreciation by use.

Furthermore, we should not endeavor to use propositions in isolation. Emphatically I do not mean, a neat little set of experiments to illustrate Proposition I and then the proof of Proposition I, a neat little set of experiments to illustrate Proposition II and then the proof of Proposition II, and so on the the end of the book. Nothing could be more boring. Interrelated truths are utilized *en bloc*, and the various propositions are employed in any order, and with any reiteration. Choose some important applications of your theoretical subject; and study them concurrently with the systematic theoretical exposition. Keep the theoretical exposition short and simple, but let it be strict and rigid so far as it goes. It should not be too long for it to be easily known with thoroughness and accuracy. The consequences of a plethora of half-digested theoretical knowledge are deplorable. Also the theory should not be muddled up with the practice. The child should have no doubt when it is proving and when it is utilizing. My point is that what is proved should be utilized, and that what is utilized should—so far as is practicable—be proved. I am far from asserting that proof and utilization are the same thing.

At this point of my discourse, I can most directly carry forward my argument in the outward form of a digression. We are only just realizing that the art and science of education require a genius and a study of their own; and that this genius and this science are more than a bare knowledge of some branch of science or of literature. This truth was partially perceived in the past generation; and headmasters, somewhat crudely, were apt to supersede learning in their colleagues by requiring left-hand bowling and a taste for football. But culture is more than cricket, and more than football, and more than extent of knowledge.

Education is the acquisition of the art of the utilization of knowledge. This is an art very difficult to impart. Whenever a textbook is written of real educational worth, you may be quite certain that some reviewer will say that it will be difficult to teach from it. Of course it will be difficult to teach from it. If it were easy, the book ought to be burned; for it cannot be educational. In education, as elsewhere, the broad primrose path leads to a nasty place. This evil path is represented by a book or a set of lectures which will practically enable the student to learn by heart all of the questions likely to be asked at the next external examination. And I may say in passing that no educational system is possible unless every question directly asked by the actual teacher of that pupil in that subject. The external assessor may report on the curriculum or on the performance of the pupils, but never should be allowed to ask the pupil a question which has not been strictly supervised by the actual teacher, or at least inspired by a long conference with him. There are a few exceptions to this rule, but they are exceptions, and could easily be allowed for under the general rule.

We now return to my previous point, that theoretical ideas should always find important applications within the pupil's curriculum. This is not an easy doctrine to apply, but a very hard one. It contains within itself the problem of keeping knowledge alive, of preventing it from becoming inert, which is the central problem of all education.

The best procedure will depend on several factors, none of which can be neglected, namely, the genius of the teacher, the intellectual type of the pupils, their prospects in life, the opportunities offered by the immediate surroundings of the school, and allied factors of this sort. It is for this reason that the uniform external examination is so deadly. We do not denounce it because we are cranks, and like denouncing established things. We are not so childish. Also, of course, such examinations have their use in testing slackness. Our reason of dislike is very definite and very practical. It kills the best part of culture. When you analyze in the light of experience the central task of education, you find that its successful accomplishment depends on a delicate adjustment of many variable factors. The reason is that we are dealing with human minds, and not with dead matter. The evocation of curiosity, of judgment, of the power of mastering a complicated tangle of circumstances, the use of theory in giving foresight in special cases—all these powers are not to be imparted by a set rule embodied in one schedule of examination subjects.

I appeal to you, as practical teachers. With good discipline, it is always possible to pump into the minds of a class a certain quantity of inert knowledge. You take a text-book and make them learn it. So far, so good. The child then knows how to solve a quadratic equation. But what is the point of teaching a child to solve a quadratic equation? There is a traditional answer to this question. It runs thus: The mind is an instrument, you first sharpen it, and then use it; the acquisition of the power of solving a quadratic equation is part of the process of sharpening the mind. Now there is just enough truth in this answer to have made it live through the ages. But for all its half-truth, it embodies a radical error which bids fair to stifle the genius of the modern world. I do not know who was first responsible for this analogy of the mind to a dead instrument. For aught I know, it may have been one of the seven wise men of Greece, or a committee of the whole lot of them. Whoever was the originator, there can be no doubt of the authority which it has acquired by the continuous approval bestowed upon it by eminent persons. But whatever its weight of authority, whatever the high approval which it can quote, I have no hesitation in denouncing it as one of the most fatal, erroneous, and dangerous conceptions ever introduced into the theory of education. The mind is never passive; it is a perpetual activity, delicate, receptive, responsive to stimulus. You cannot postpone its life until you have sharpened it. Whatever interest attaches to your subject-matter must be evoked here and now; whatever powers you are strengthening in the pupil, must be exercised here and now; whatever possibilities of mental life your teaching should impart, must be exhibited here and now. That is the golden rule of education, and a very difficult rule to follow.

The difficulty is just this: the apprehension of general ideas, intellectual habits of mind, and pleasurable interest in mental achievement can be evoked by no form of words, however accurately adjusted. All practical teachers know that education is a patient process of the mastery of details, minute by minute, hour by hour, day by day. There is no royal road to learning through an airy path of brilliant generalizations. There is a proverb about the difficulty of seeing the wood because of the trees. That difficulty is exactly the point which I am enforcing. The problem of education is to make the pupil see the wood by means of the trees.

The solution which I am urging, is to eradicate the fatal disconnection of subjects which kills the vitality of our modern curriculum. There is only one subject-matter for education, and that is Life in all its manifestations. Instead of this single unity, we offer children—Algebra, from which nothing follows; Geometry, from which nothing follows; Science, from which nothing follows; History, from which nothing follows; a Couple of Languages, never mastered; and lastly, most dreary of all, Literature, represented by plays of Shakespeare, with philological notes and short analyses of plot and character to be in substance committed to memory. Can such a list be said to represent Life, as it is known in the midst of the living of it? The best that can be said of it is, that it is a rapid table of contents which a deity might run over in his mind while he was thinking of creating a world, and has not yet determined how to put it together.

Let us now return to quadratic equations. We still have on hand the unanswered question. Why should children be taught their solution? Unless quadratic equations fit into a connected curriculum, of course there is no reason to teach anything about them. Furthermore, extensive as should be the place of mathematics in a complete culture, I am a little doubtful whether for many types of boys algebraic solutions of quadratic equations do not lie on the specialist side of mathematics. I may here remind you that as yet I have not said anything of the psychology or the content of the specialism, which is so necessary a part of an ideal education. But all that is an evasion of our real question, and I merely state it in order to avoid being misunderstood in my answer.

Quadratic equations are part of algebra, and algebra is the intellectual instrument which has been created for rendering clear the quantitative aspects of the world. There is no getting out of it. Through and through, the world is infected with quantity. To talk sense, is to talk in quantities. It is no use saying that the nation is large,—How large? It is no use saying that radium is scarce,—How scarce? You cannot evade quantity. You may fly to poetry and to music, and quantity and number will face you in your rhythms and your octaves. Elegant intellects which despise the theory of quantity, are but half developed. They are more to be pitied than blamed. The scraps of gibberish, which in their school-days were taught to them in the name of algebra, deserve some contempt.

This question of the degeneration of algebra into gibberish, both in word and in fact, affords a pathetic instance of the uselessness of reforming educational schedules without a clear conception of the attributes which you wish to evoke in the living minds of the children. A few years ago there was an outcry that school algebra was in need of reform, but there was a general agreement that graphs would put everything right. So all sorts of things were extruded, and graphs were introduced. So far as I can see, with no sort of idea behind them, but just graphs. Now every examination paper has one or two questions on graphs. Personally I am an enthusiastic adherent of graphs. But I wonder whether as yet we have gained very much. You cannot put life into any schedule of general education unless you succeed in exhibiting its relation to some essential characteristic of all intelligent or emotional perception. It is a hard saying, but it is true; and I do not see how to make it any easier. In making these little formal alterations you are beaten by the very nature of things. You are pitted against too skillful an adversary who will see to it that the pea is always under the other thimble.

Reformation must begin at the other end. First, you must make up your mind as to those quantitative aspects of the world which are simple enough to be introduced into general education; then a schedule of algebra should be framed which will about find its exemplification in these applications. We need not fear for our pet graphs, they will be there in plenty when we once begin to treat algebra as a serious means of studying the world. Some of the simplest applications will be found in the quantities which occur in the simplest study of society. The curves of history are more vivid and more informing than the dry catalogues of names and dates which comprise the greater part of that arid school study. What purpose is effected by a catalogue of undistinguished kings and queens? Tom, Dick, or Harry, they are all dead. General resurrections are failures, and are better postponed. The quantitative flux of the forces of modern society is capable of very simple exhibition. Meanwhile, the idea of the variable, of the function, of rate of change, of equations and their solution, of elimination, are being studied as an abstract science for their own sake. Not, of course, in the pompous phrases with which I am alluding to them here, but with that iteration of simple special cases proper to teaching.

If this course be followed, the route from Chaucer to the Black Death, from the Black Death to modern Labor troubles, will connect the tales of the medieval pilgrims with the abstract science of algebra, both yielding diverse aspects of that single theme, Life. I know what most of you are thinking at this point. It is that the exact course which I have sketched out is not the particular one which you would have chosen, or even seen how to work. I quite agree. I am not claiming that I could do it myself. But your objection is the precise reason why a common external examination system is fatal to education. The process of exhibiting the applications of knowledge must, for its success, essentially depend on the character of the pupils and the genius of the teacher. Of course I have left out the easiest applications with which most of us are more at home. I mean the quantitative sides of sciences, such as mechanics and physics.

Again, in the same connection we plot the statistics of social phenomena against the time. We then eliminate the time between suitable pairs. We can speculate how far we have exhibited a real causal connection, or how far a mere temporal coincidence. We notice that we might have plotted against the time one set of statistics for one country, and another set for another country, and thus, with suitable choice of subjects, have obtained graphs which certainly exhibited mere coincidence. Also other graphs exhibit obvious causal connections. We wonder how to discriminate. And so are drawn on as far as we will.

But in considering this description, I must beg you to remember what I have been insisting on above. In the first place, one train of thought will not suit all groups of children. For example, I should expect that artisan children will want something more concrete and, in a sense, swifter than I have set down here. Perhaps I am wrong, but that is what I should guess. In the second place, I am not contemplating one beautiful lecture stimulating, once and for all, an admiring class. That is not the way in which education proceeds. No; all the time, the pupils are hard at work solving examples, drawing graphs, and making experiments, until they have a thorough hold on the whole subject. I am describing the interspersed explanations, the directions which should be given to their thoughts. The pupils have got to be made to feel that they are studying something, and are not merely executing intellectual minuets.

Finally, if you are teaching pupils for some general examination, the problem of sound teaching is greatly complicated. Have you ever noticed the zig-zag moulding round a Norman arch? The ancient work is beautiful, the modern work is hideous. The reason is, that the modern work is done to exact measure, the ancient work is varied according to the idiosyncrasy of the workman. Here it is crowded, and there it is expanded. Now the essence of getting pupils through examinations is to give equal weight to all parts of the schedule. But mankind is naturally specialist. One man sees a whole subject, where another can find only a few detached examples. I know that it seems contradictory to allow for specialism in a curriculum especially designed for a broad culture. Without contradictions the world would be simpler, and perhaps duller. But I am certain that in education wherever you exclude specialism you destroy life.

We now come to the other great branch of a general mathematical education, namely Geometry. The same principles apply. The theoretical part should be clear-cut, rigid, short, and important. Every proposition not absolutely necessary to exhibit the main connection of ideas should be cut out, but the great fundamental ideas should be all there. No omission of concepts, such as those of Similarity and Proportion. We must remember that, owing to the aid rendered by the visual presence of a figure, Geometry is a field of unequalled excellence for the exercise of the deductive faculties of reasoning. Then, of course, there follows Geometrical Drawing, with its training for the hand and eye.

But, like Algebra, Geometry and Geometrical Drawing must be extended beyond the mere circle of geometrical ideas. In an industrial neighborhood, machinery and workshop practice form the appropriate extension. For example, in the London Polytechnics this has been achieved with conspicuous success. For many secondary schools I suggest that surveying and maps are the natural applications. In particular, plane-table surveying should lead pupils to a vivid apprehension of the immediate application of geometric truths. Simple drawing apparatus, a surveyor's chain, and a surveyor's compass, should enable the pupils to rise from the survey and mensuration of a field to the construction of the map of a small district. The best education is to be found in gaining the utmost information from the simplest apparatus. The provision of elaborate instruments is greatly to be deprecated. To have constructed the map of a small district, to have considered its roads, its contours, its geology, its climate, its relation to other districts, the effects on the status of its inhabitants, will teach more history and geography than any knowledge of Perkin Warbeck or of Behren's Straits. I mean not a nebulous lecture on the subject, but a serious investigation in which the real facts are definitely ascertained by the aid of accurate theoretical knowledge. A typical mathematical problem should be: Survey such and such a field, draw a plan of it to such and such a scale, and find the area. It would be quite a good procedure to impart the necessary geometrical propositions without their proofs. Then, concurrently in the same term, the proofs of the propositions would be learnt while the survey was being made.

Fortunately, the specialist side of education presents an easier problem than does the provision of a general culture. For this there are many reasons. One is that many of the principles of procedure to be observed are the same in both cases, and it is unnecessary to recapitulate. Another reason is that specialist training takes place—or should take place—at a more advanced stage of the pupil's course, and thus there is easier material to work upon. But undoubtedly the chief reason is that the specialist study is normally a study of peculiar interest to the student. He is studying it because, for some reason, he wants to know it. This makes all the difference. The general culture is designed to foster an activity of mind; the specialist course utilizes this activity. But it does not do to lay too much stress on these neat antitheses. As we have already seen, in the general course foci of special interest will arise; and similarly in the special study, the external connections of the subject drag thought outwards.

Again, there is not one course of study which merely gives general culture, and another which gives special knowledge. The subjects pursued for the sake of a general education are special subjects specially studied; and, on the other hand, one of the ways of encouraging general mental activity is to foster a special devotion. You may not divide the seamless coat of learning. What education has to impart is an intimate sense for the power of ideas, for the beauty of ideas, and for the structure of ideas, together with a particular body of knowledge which has peculiar reference to the life of the being possessing it.

The appreciation of the structure of ideas is that side of a cultured mind which can only grow under the influence of a special study. I mean that eye for the whole chess-board, for the bearing of one set of ideas on another. Nothing but a special study can give any appreciation for the exact formulation of general ideas, for their relations when formulated, for their service in the comprehension of life. A mind so disciplined should be both more abstract and more concrete. It has been trained in the comprehension of abstract thought and in the analysis of facts.

Finally, there should grow the most austere of all mental qualities; I mean the sense for style. It is an aesthetic sense, based on admiration for the direct attainment of a foreseen end, simply and without waste. Style in art, style in literature, style in science, style in logic, style in practical execution have fundamentally the same aesthetic qualities, namely, attainment and restraint. The love of a subject in itself and for itself, where it is not the sleepy pleasure of pacing a mental quarterdeck, is the love of style as manifested in that study.

Here we are brought back to the position from which we started, the utility of education. Style, in its finest sense, is the last acquirement of the educated mind; it is also the most useful. It pervades the whole being. The administrator with a sense for style hates waste; the engineer with a sense for style economizes his material; the artisan with a sense for style prefers good work. Style is the ultimate morality of mind.

But above style, and above knowledge, there is something, a vague shape like fate above the Greek gods. That something is Power. Style is the fashioning of power, the restraining of power. But, after all, the power of attainment of the desired end is fundamental. The first thing is to get there. Do not bother about your style, but solve your problem, justify the ways of God to man, administer your province, or do whatever else is set before you.

Where, then, does style help? In this, with style the end is attained without side issues, without raising undesirable inflammations. With style you attain your end and nothing but your end. With style the effect of your activity is calculable, and foresight is the last gift of gods to men. With style your power is increased, for your mind is not distracted with irrelevancies, and you are more likely to attain your object. Now style is the exclusive privilege of the expert. Whoever heard of the style of an amateur painter, of the style of an amateur poet? Style is always the product of specialist study, the peculiar contribution of specialism to culture.

English education in its present phase suffers from a lack of definite aim, and from an external machinery which kills its vitality. Hitherto in this address I have been considering the aims which should govern education. In this respect England halts between two opinions. It has not decided whether to produce amateurs or experts. The profound change in the world which the nineteenth century has produced is that the growth of knowledge has given foresight. The amateur is essentially a man with appreciation and with immense versatility in mastering a given routine. But he lacks the foresight which comes from special knowledge. The object of this address is to suggest how to produce the expert without loss of the essential virtues of the amateur. The machinery of our secondary education is rigid where it should be yielding, and lax where it should be rigid. Every school is bound on pain of extinction to train its boys for a small set of definite examinations. No headmaster has a free hand to develop his general education or his specialist studies in accordance with the opportunities of his school, which are created by its staff, its environment, its class of boys, and its endowments. I suggest that no system of external tests which aims primarily at examining individual scholars can result in anything but educational waste.

Primarily it is the schools and not the scholars which should be inspected. Each school should grant its own leaving certificates, based on its own curriculum. The standards of these schools should be sampled and corrected. But the first requisite for educational reform is the school as a unit, with its approved curriculum based on its own needs, and evolved by its own staff. If we fail to secure that, we simply fall from one formalism into another, from one dung-hill of inert ideas into another.

In stating that the school is the true educational unit in any national system for the safeguarding of efficiency, I have conceived the alternative system as being the external examination of the individual scholar. But every Scylla is faced by its Charybdis—or, in more homely language, there is a ditch on both sides of the road. It will be equally fatal to education if we fall into the hands of a supervising department which is under the impression that it can divide all schools into two or three rigid categories, each type being forced to adopt a rigid curriculum. When I say that the school is the educational unit, I mean exactly what I say, no larger unit, no smaller unit. Each school must have the claim to be considered in relation to its special circumstances. The classifying of schools for some purposes is necessary. But no absolutely rigid curriculum, not modified by its own staff, should be permissible. Exactly the same principles apply, with the proper modifications, to universities and to technical colleges.

When one considers in its length and in its breadth the importance of this question of the education of a nation's young, the broken lives, the defeated hopes, the national failures, which result from the frivolous inertia with which it is treated, it is difficult to restrain within oneself a savage rage. In the conditions of modern life the rule is absolute, the race which does not value trained intelligence is doomed. Not all your heroism, not all your social charm, not all your wit, not all your victories on land or at sea, can move back the finger of fate. Today we maintain ourselves. Tomorrow science will have moved forward yet one more step, and there will be no appeal from the judgment which will then be pronounced on the uneducated.

We can be content with no less than the old summary of educational ideal which has been current at any time from the dawn of our civilization. The essence of education is that it be religious.

Pray, what is religious education?

A religious education is an education which inculcates duty and reverence. Duty arises from our potential control over the course of events. Where attainable knowledge could have changed the issue, ignorance has the guilt of vice. And the foundation of reverence is this perception, that the present holds within itself the complete sum of existence, backwards and forwards, that whole amplitude of time, which is eternity.

HOWARD OZMON is presently the Chairman of the Department of Education at Chicago State College. He attended the University of Virginia and received a doctorate from Columbia University. His other books include *The Philosophical Development of Educational Thought*, *Challenging Ideas in Education*, *Twelve Great Philosophers*, *Dewey's Philosophy*, and *Utopias and Education*. He is listed in the *Directory of American Philosophers* and *Who's Who in America*.

46,897